M
22.95

In Addition
to Tuition

In Addition to Tuition

The Parents' Survival Guide to Freshman Year of College

Marian Edelman Borden
Mary Anne Burlinson
Elsie R. Kearns

Facts On File®

AN INFOBASE HOLDINGS COMPANY

In Addition to Tuition: The Parents' Survival Guide to Freshman Year of College

Facts On File, Inc.
460 Park Avenue South
New York NY 10016

Library of Congress Cataloging-in-Publication Data

Borden, Marian Edelman.
   In addition to tuition: the parents' survival guide to freshman year of college/by Marian Edelman Borden, Mary Anne
Burlinson, Elsie R. Kearns.
      p. cm.
   Includes index.
   ISBN 0-8160-3099-5 (acid-free paper) 0-8160-3341-2 (paperback)
   1. College student orientation—United States. 2. College students—United States—Family relationships. I. Burlinson, Mary Anne. II. Kearns, Elsie R. III. Title.
LB2343.32.B67 1995
378.1'98—dc20   94–41725

Facts On File books are available at special discounts when purchased in bulk quantities for businesses, associations, institutions, or sales promotions. Please call our Special Sales Department in New York at 212/683-2244 or 800/322-8755.

Jacket design by Carla Weise

Printed in the United States of America

MP FOF 10 9 8 7 6 5 4 3 2 1

This book is printed on acid-free paper.

To Carol and Evelyn P. Edelman,
parents extraordinaire;
and *of course* John.—M.E.B.

To R.F.B., with whom I share my empty nest.
—M.A.B.

To Tom, Susan, Matthew, and Anne Marie:
What Dreams
Are Made Of.—E.R.K.

CONTENTS

1. Getting Your Act Together—and Taking It on the Road

Going away to camp was nothing compared to the kind of operation involved in setting up headquarters away from home. Here are the logistics of purchasing, packing, and getting everything there, including clothes, linens, computers, electrical gadgets, and electronic equipment. There are also tips about campus security and about bringing student cars to campus.

2. You Can Bank on It

Dollars and Sense—you'll need plenty of both during this year. Here's a financial primer for paying the bills—from budgeting to tuition plans, loans, and student jobs—and accessing the money on campus via checking accounts, ATMs, and credit cards.

3. In Sickness and in Health

The student away from home doesn't stop getting sick, needing doctors and dentists, glasses, hospitals, and insurance coverage—nor will he be isolated from issues involving alcohol, sex, and emotional problems. Here are suggestions for dealing with your child's physical and mental well-being.

4. Living with Strangers: An Arranged Marriage

They may not be choosing a partner for life, but students can certainly be affected by roommates during that first year at school. Here is a discussion about different living arrangements—from the number of roommates to the kinds of dorms—along with tips for getting along with roommates and what to do if it doesn't work.

5. Setting Up Shop

For better or for worse, the parents usually make that first moving-in trip. Here are answers to the questions about who's going, how to get there, what happens when you do, and when to leave, as well as suggestions for setting up the room. The question of whose nest is it—the child's or the parent's—is also tackled here.

6. Staying Connected: The Ties That Bind

Out of sight, but certainly not out of mind. Here's some advice for making the most of those long-distance calls and for handling homesickness and emotional crises at a distance. This chapter includes ideas about the expectations and realities of Parents' Weekend and for keeping in touch through care packages for every important event from birthdays to exams, as well as just an "I'm-thinking-of-you day."

7. Life Goes On

The room is empty—how are things at his "permanent home address," and what's he doing on campus? Here's a look at life for parents and siblings left behind, along with a serious—and not so serious—look at what happens when the child leaves the nest and when he comes home. The chapter has information about what his life at college might be like—including grades, religion, fraternities, romance, date rape, and sexual harassment.

8. Moving On: Caught Between Two Worlds

Plans for sophomore year begin before freshman year is even half over. Here are some tips for the future: sophomore courses and roommates, off-campus housing, transferring (if they hate the school), and summer jobs; and for tying up all those loose (and not so loose) ends—friends and relationships left behind, packing everything up, and heading home again.

PREFACE

"Of course, you'll need extra-long twin sheets." This book was born in response to that offhand comment. Two of us had never sent a child off to college, and frankly we'd been so wrapped up in the application process that we hadn't begun to think beyond it. Perhaps there would be more to this than we'd imagined—there was, much more.

Parents used to rely on word-of-mouth and trial-and-error to figure out how to get everything done. Mistakes, often costly in terms of dollars and emotion, were shrugged off to inexperience; the assumption that the process was going to be a nightmare became a self-fulfilling prophecy. *In Addition to Tuition* is our attempt to correct such a situation, to provide a step-by-step guidebook that will take you from the time your child receives a college acceptance letter through freshman year—and to do it in such a way that the parent-child relationship is enhanced.

We have included factual information in the text, as well as in the form of bulleted listings, boldfaced tips, boxed material, and appendices. However, you'll find that there is often no single right answer to some of your questions—so we've also presented the advantages and disadvantages of the various alternatives.

Beyond the mechanics, however, we were struck by how much emotion is involved during this first college year: knowing what to say to your child, how to say it, and when. We've presented here material you should find helpful in having your own "conversations with campus." Each chapter stands as an entity unto itself—you can read from cover to cover or choose sections that are pertinent to whatever stage of the process you're in. The stories within the text run the gamut from serious to amusing—tales of what has happened to other parents and their children, all intended to make you wiser from the start.

We wrote this book for parents, from the parents' perspective. There's nothing in it, however, that your student can't or shouldn't read. In fact, we received a high accolade from one of our children who wrote, "It's great to see that despite generation gaps, you've captured a lot of what college students feel and think. It makes me believe that parents and their children can communicate meaningfully."

As the mothers of four daughters and six sons, we are firmly committed to gender equality. The issue of which pronoun to use troubled us, but we finally decided, for the sake of consistency, clarity, and limited space, to refer to students as *he* rather than using masculine and feminine pronouns in alternating chapters or the cumbersome *he or she*. Clearly, this book is for our daughters, as well as our sons.

The word freshman has also become politically charged, and many institutions now use the term "first-year student" for the sake of gender equality. Most parents, however, are familiar with the word freshman from their own college days, and the two terms are still used interchangeably in many campus publications—thus, you'll find both in the text.

Throughout the book we've often used the phrase *your child*. This is a book written by mothers, and we felt that although your freshman may now be a young adult, he will always be *your child*. While the first year of college is a continuing process of your letting go and recognizing his growing maturity, and of his assumption of responsibility, nonetheless he still very much needs his parents and you need to continue to function in that role.

We have many people to thank: Our families, especially our husbands, Robert Burlinson, Tom Kearns, and John Borden, who supported this project and offered advice, perspective, and editorial suggestions. We are indebted to our children: Susan, Matthew, and Anne Marie Kearns; Bob, Kate, and Andrew Burlinson; and Charles, Sam, Dan, and Maggie Borden. You are our inspirations.

Special thanks to the many students, parents, and college administrators from around the country whom we interviewed for this book. Your honesty and perspective will help make the adjustment to college much easier for other families.

We are very grateful to the administration and counseling staff of Mamaroneck High School, Mamaroneck, New York, and most especially to Ellie Fredston and Marie Ruggiero in the MHS Financial Aid Office. Their experience, and especially Marie's wonderful sense of humor, were invaluable during the year that this book went from idea to reality. We offer sincere gratitude to Kay Gill, Richard Amundson, Dr. Ralph Candela, Kirby Candela, and Dr. Neil LeLeiko for their helpful suggestions for the chapter on student health; and to Bill Burig for his comments on housing and roommates in chapter four. Our thanks to Kate Kelly for her help with the original book proposal. We also appreciate the stories, perspective, and good humor we received from Frances Flanagan and the boys in Weld 33.

We value the counsel and support of our agent, Jim Levine; his assistant, Arielle Eckstadt; and most especially, our editor, Randy Ladenheim-Gil, who believed in this project and shared our vision of this book.

To those parents in the midst of sending a child off to college, good luck. It's a scary time—but one of the most fulfilling, exciting, satisfying periods of your life . . . and we lived to tell the tale.

IN THE BEGINNING . . .

Congratulations! Your child is in . . . accepted to college! You've survived the application process, the months of waiting, the tension of making decisions. You've mailed the deposit and sealed the commitment. He's definitely going—in fact, there are days when you wonder whether he's already out the door, at least mentally.

He's floating on cloud nine, but you're starting to wonder why *you* should be excited. Your child is leaving home, and you're paying tens of thousands of dollars over four years to help him leave. You're having attacks of separation anxiety, and you haven't even separated. You've been told there will be a ton of things to do, and you don't even know what they are yet. It should be a breeze to pack up the next child and ship him off to college when it's his turn—but this one is the grand experiment, and you're still not ready to work in the lab.

Whatever you're feeling, however much you want *not* to feel, the fact is that the world out there is about to become your child's new playground—and you're going to be dealing with your own set of roller-coaster emotions. The ride is just beginning. . . .

GETTING YOUR ACT | 1
TOGETHER—AND TAKING IT
ON THE ROAD

"It's been 25 years since I was in college, and I went off with a portable typewriter, four pairs of chinos, two sweaters, and a navy blue sports jacket. My daughter's bare essentials included summer, fall, and winter clothes—she said she'd pick up the spring wardrobe when she came home for Christmas—plus one CD player·and two speakers, a computer and printer, answering machine, books, cosmetics, shampoo for a year, sheets, towels, and a comforter. Try getting all that plus my wife, my daughter, and myself into a compact car! I thought getting her into school was the tough part, but literally getting her off to school was a lot harder than I'd imagined."

In some ways sending your child off to college resembles planning a wedding and setting the newlyweds up in their first apartment. The student may buy new clothes, sheets, and towels (a trousseau?) and is full of ideas for decorating a new living space (the dorm room), while you're wrestling with a barrage of forms and other details. It can be an exciting (and will be an expensive) time. On the other hand it can be difficult. In a less-than-charitable mood, one frustrated father remarked, "Sending my daughter to school was like moving an army division into battle." Planning requires organization and patience.

But there's more going on than just shopping, packing, and filling out forms. The trips to the mall, the debates over comforters, the questions over how much shampoo to take or whether it makes more sense to buy the same brand when you get there—all of it is part of the separation process, and that can make it hard.

You might prefer to view your child's departure for college as temporary, somewhat like a family vacation. But, realistically, it's not. During those summer weeks, your emotions—and those of your freshman—probably run the gamut: worry, excitement, fear, curiosity. You may find days when it's difficult to exchange a civil word to each other—a frustrating situation because it's also a time you want to cherish. Ironically, anger is one way your child may express his conflicting feelings about leaving, and he may be less than helpful when you try to figure out what—or how much—to take.

Adding to the tension is the pressure of so many other decisions to be made in a short period of time. On the plus side, all the activity helps mask the parental feelings of loss that begin to grow. After the packing is done and the last form is filled out, your child's room probably looks stripped and bare—and the reality of his leaving home hits you.

A PAPER BLIZZARD

"I thought my son would eat many of his weekend meals off-campus, so I limited the amount of his meal plan. When he ended up eating at the dorm most of the time, he had to make friends with the football players who had unlimited food and he sponged off them."

"It was a lot more walking than I ever thought possible." (Reaction of a dirty and very tired freshman returning from his orientation hiking trip.)

Once your child has made his decision, a ton of mail arrives from college and most of it needs a response. Here are some suggestions:

- Keep all the material together in a file folder or box.
- Carefully note the various deadlines; mark when you return each document.
- Keep a copy of school-related canceled checks in this folder for easy reference.

Feeding Frenzy

One of the forms that will cross your desk is the food plan signup. Don't automatically assume that your child will eat three square meals a day, nor that he will eat all those meals on campus. Do you have options? Some schools mandate that students enroll in the college meal plan for a set fee—and it's irrelevant whether your child chooses to eat three hearty meals a day or never sees the inside of a dining hall the entire year. While you might reasonably point out that you're paying for the food ("Could he please eat some of it?"), under this system you pay whether he eats or not.

Other schools offer options: Some allow you to enroll for fewer meals; others permit parents to pay a varying amount, and each student meal eaten is deducted from a campus account. You must make an educated guess about how much to deposit into this account. Before making a decision, consider:

- Has the school provided any guidelines for making a choice? (average meal plan for varsity athlete? for men? for women?)
- Suppose your option is inadequate for the first term: can your child add to the meal plan or account?
- Can you change your selection for the next term?
- What happens to any unused portion?
- If the leftover amount is returned in the form of a check to your child, be sure he doesn't use this as an incentive to skimp on meals.

Involve your child in the decision about a meal plan. He should know what the selection means in terms of how he eats on campus and what, if any, effect it has on the quantity he can eat at one sitting. (Is it "an all-you-can-eat buffet" or is there a charge for seconds?) If he knows you have already paid for breakfast, he might be more inclined to take advantage of it instead of going elsewhere for a doughnut in the middle of the morning.

Unfortunately, unless your child has had a previous opportunity to spend some time on campus, neither of you can be sure that he is going to like the food that is available—it can be like going to a pot-luck supper. Part of his college experience may be the necessity of eating foods he's never tried or isn't particularly fond of.

Realistically, you won't necessarily know what—or how well—your child is eating. As one freshman confessed to his mother at the end of the year, "Remember all those salads I told you I was eating . . .?"

Summer Orientation Programs

Student orientation isn't just for the first week of school anymore. Some colleges bring in their freshmen in small groups over the summer; other schools offer a choice of orientation programs to meet the needs of different interests or groups. Before you make family vacation plans or your child commits to a summer job schedule, contact the college for the dates of mandatory and optional orientation programs.

An increasingly popular type of preorientation is a hiking/camping trip. A small group of freshmen, led by upperclassmen, spend several days on the road getting to know each other in an informal setting. If your student enjoys the great outdoors, this can be a lot of fun.

Many students who have participated in these trips have wonderful memories of them and forge lasting friendships during them. But insist that your child be realistic: if he is a novice camper, be sure to check how challenging the trip will be. If the conditions are less than ideal (rain, heat, cold) and the terrain is difficult, will your child enjoy the experience? This may be his first introduction to a group of fellow students: What will their impression of him be? Someone who tries his best with good humor—or an irritating whiner? Will it bother him to arrive on campus covered with trail dust or late for move-in? There's no need to feel that any particular orientation experience is the right one for everyone.

Academic Decisions

Your child will receive a course catalog before school starts. Some colleges register for the first term by mail. Others offer special, select courses for which a freshman must apply in the summer. If he is accepted, it will dictate the rest of his schedule.

While some schools have a rigid core curriculum and freshman choices are limited, most colleges offer a wide array of classes, and the very breadth of selection may be frightening. How can your child make intelligent decisions about courses that are just descriptions in a book, especially when he's not on campus? What advice can you give him?

First, if he visits the campus after acceptance, suggest that he check out some of the curriculum offerings by sitting in on classes. One high school senior used her prefrosh days (the visiting days in the spring at school for students who have been admitted) to ask the college students she met about the courses they were taking:

- Who were the teachers to seek out—and the ones to avoid?
- Should she take the course she was academically qualified for—or the lower-level one?
- Which courses require heavy reading? heavy writing?

Your child might also check the college library or bookstore for a student-produced "course evaluation guide"—remembering to take any extreme comments with a grain of salt. The bookstore might also be divided by course offering, and your child can get an advance look at the kind of text and/or supplementary reading needed.

Keep in mind that a student's high school preparation in an academic area might not reflect how he does in a particular college course. One student found that although he had excelled in languages in high school, he wasn't nearly fluent enough to hold his own at the advanced level in college. Departments within a school can vary, too: a supposed introductory course may provide a wonderful foundation or be so complicated that previous knowledge is a must. The dullest subject can be made fascinating with the right teacher, but a boring professor can kill the most interesting topic. One student found that one of his best classes was an introduction to Latin taught by a terrific teaching assistant! Parents tend to worry about whether a child is being taught by a full professor—yet, students often prefer the teaching assistants because they are closer in age and more approachable.

If your child doesn't have access to the campus ahead of time, he should call an academic advisor there with any questions he may have. At some schools there is a "shopping period" during which students "check out" courses before actually enrolling in them. In any case, there is usually the option of dropping one course and adding another within a specified time period at the beginning of the term.

It's important that both you and the student read through the course catalog when it comes. (Call the school if the catalog doesn't arrive before you leave. Find out if it's lost or just late.) Ideally, this is the time for some serious conversations between parents and child—not just about immediate course selections, but also about the big academic picture over the next four years. Even if your student insists on making all these decisions on his own, it is a good idea at least to familiarize yourself with the course offerings, so that you can better understand what is happening scholastically and can make intelligent suggestions if there is a problem.

Most schools have distribution requirements for graduation that dictate that a student must take a certain number of courses in a variety of disciplines, as well as a greater number of classes in his chosen major. While some students enter college with very definite ideas about what they want to do when they graduate—and therefore have a clear plan of what courses are necessary—the majority of freshmen are vague about their future. Freshman year (and to a certain extent, sophomore year) is designed to permit students to sample from the various departments of the college before choosing a major.

The decision about which courses to take will ultimately belong to your child, but he may not have the perspective and distance to balance his class schedule.

REMEMBER: First semester is a time of adjustment. While no one is suggesting that your student should take all "gut" courses, this is no time to overload him either.

Other Forms

Your student will also receive medical forms and information from the college about health services (see Chapter 3). He'll be asked to complete a questionnaire on roommate preferences, and he'll probably receive the names and addresses of his roommate(s) before he gets to campus (see Chapter 5). Local banks and credit-card companies will send their own literature (see Chapter 2). Your student may have the opportunity to join, before arriving on campus, an organization affiliated with your religion (if you've designated one on your application), as well as other extracurricular activities. The college may also send out housing regulations and contracts, notification and rules about move-in day, and information about Parents' Weekend and campus publications. Don't make any decisions hastily in an attempt to deal with all the paperwork. (See Appendix G for a sampling of the wide variety of student groups on campus.)

PLAN AHEAD, TAKE INVENTORY

"My daughter was going to be a counselor at a sleep-away camp. The only time we could shop was in June, the week between the end of exams and graduation."

"There we were in the store, my son walking at least 2 feet behind me while I was chattering away about coordinating towel colors. Finally, he said in exasperation, 'Who cares if the towels match? Nobody but me is going to see them.'"

It's an exciting adventure, albeit an expensive one, to buy everything new for college. But, of course, there's no rule that all the towels, sheets, and comforters have to be recently purchased. In fact, it might even be reassuring to have some familiar items from home in the dorm. So look over the lists and decide *before* you start for the mall what you will buy and what you will bring from your own linen closet. Given the explosion in catalog shopping, if you prefer, many purchases can be made without leaving your living room.

Realistically, consider the size of the dorm room and the closet space. Then add the number of roommates and divide accordingly. The quarters rarely are spacious. Squeezing too many articles of clothing and other items into a limited space with one or more roommates can create friction before you even get properly introduced.

TIP: "When in doubt, leave it home." You can always send additional clothes and equipment later.

When you shop may be a function of your family's schedules, your own style, and your distance from school. Similar to shopping for the holidays, some families prefer to do one shopping blitz two weeks (two days?) before the start of school, while others slowly accumulate what they need over several months. It's fine to wait until the end, but keep in mind that this is a busy, emotionally difficult period when your child may want to spend time with his high school friends rather than in the stores.

If your student will be going to a college that is a considerable distance from home, one alternative is to go to school a few days early, stay in a nearby motel, and purchase the bulk of the necessities there. You'll avoid the packing and transporting hassles, and even if you end up buying merchandise at a premium, the savings in shipping fees may be worth it.

Some students prefer to shop with friends or even on their own. It may be their first real opportunity to express their taste and independence, and parental suggestions may or may not be welcome. Other students show little interest, preferring to leave the decisions to parents. Understanding your child's motivations will help you decide what your role should be in the process. If he shows no interest in preparing for college, it may be a sign of anxiety about separating from home. Talking through his concerns and offering reassurance and support may help. On the other hand, this dearth of interest could also be a genuine lack of concern about what towels he takes, just so long as he has towels!

THE CLOTHES LINE

"The summer before she left for college, my daughter turned an unused room into her own personal department store—piled up all the clothes she owned in her past life and all her new purchases. Seemed like she was preparing never to return."

"After my son got to campus, he turned to me and said that he had brought the wrong clothes."

Although some students see the college experience as an opportunity to throw out the old and bring on the new, most will pack what they have and add extra pieces, either before they go or while they are there. One student really did pack everything she owned—including clothes she never wore much at home. Result? She never wore the stuff at school either, a bitter time- (and space-) consuming lesson.

Here are a few guidelines:

- How soon will the seasons change where your student is going?
- If he will be coming home before the weather turns, can he bring the next season's wardrobe back with him? Or will there be time for you to send it later? Remember: Whatever he brings, he will have to store it in a limited amount of space.
- Is the campus near a shopping center (to which he has easy access)? Before buying so many new clothes at home, he may want to wait until he sees what others are wearing. Don't forget about catalog shopping—name-brand catalogs are favorite reading around dorms and also save figuring out how to get it all there yourself.
- Does your student play a sport or participate in other strenuous activity? Students who do are going to use more outfits per day than those who don't.
- How often will your student do the wash? Don't expect a weekly commitment, but don't think you have to budget for and send supplies to last a month.
- Remember, too: All that dirty laundry must be stored (or piled) somewhere in his room.

Basic Wardrobe

Shopping for college is similar to shopping for any trip, except that the time spent away from home may be longer. This list will get you started and help you avoid some common mistakes. The number indicated for some categories represents total need. You might want to reduce those numbers to allow for purchases of school-logo clothes. One freshman arrived at college with a full supply of shirts, but wound up buying a T-shirt from every "cause" on campus, eventually stuffing everything into small bulging drawers. (See Appendix A for checklist.)

- Underwear and socks. Number one on the list—you can never send enough. It's not absurd to send 18 sets, and two dozen may come in handy. As one freshman quickly learned, "During exams, he who has the most socks and underwear gets the best grades. There's no time to do wash."
- Shirts. For the child who goes through a couple of shirts a day, 24 is not farfetched—less than a two-week supply—and don't forget about layering! This, of course, is a combination of T-shirts and others he may wear. Note: If your child is used to wearing 100 percent cotton, either straight from the ironing board or professionally done, realize that it may be worn wrinkled or, more likely, not worn at all. Before loading up with what will only hang in a closet, look for synthetic fibers that will stand up to college life— or make sure that your student can iron or is willing to pay to have his shirts professionally pressed.
- Pants, sweaters, sweatshirts. Don't expect these to be washed (or cleaned) as often, and don't make the mistake of packing too many. Students tend to have their favorite pieces and will often wear them almost exclusively—especially because you will not be there to snatch items for the wash.
- Shoes. Even if the shoe of choice is the sneaker, be sure there is an extra pair or two in case one gets soaked in the rain, worn out, or lost. Your child will probably also need a couple of other kinds of shoes or boots, depending on the weather and styles.

- Outerwear. Know the climate and pack accordingly! If temperatures will dip below freezing shortly after your child's arrival on campus, be sure that he has more than a fall windbreaker with him. Remember to pack a hat and gloves.
- Raingear. However much rain there may be at school, don't rush out to buy something your child will never wear. The great rainsuit that is guaranteed to keep him dry in a monsoon will probably sit in the closet unless he is used to wearing one at home. Remember: Your child is moving out for awhile, but he is bringing his likes and dislikes with him. If he has never used an umbrella, don't expect him to start now.
- Robes, pajamas, slippers, etc. Again, your child will carry with him the habits of a lifetime. He is not suddenly going to wear a full set of pajamas if he sleeps in sweats and boxers at home, no matter how embarrassing you find his bedtime attire. One mother was amused when all the parents ran out to buy robes for their sons because the bathrooms were coed—she didn't think they would be worn (and she was right).
- **Don't forget hangers!** The college does not supply them.

What About Dressier Clothes?

There may be occasions when your student will want more than his everyday clothes. Your son will need a more formal jacket and tie, and your daughter will wear a fancier outfit. Some campuses are, in fact, dressier than others.

Before deciding whether to pack many of these clothes with the rest of your student's belongings, think about how much they will be used, how soon, and where they will be kept. You can always send more on request, and it is also very common to borrow clothes from roommates and friends for special occasions. A tuxedo can usually be rented near campus.

Jewelry: Just Another Box?

Whatever your personal opinions about jewelry on campus, you will quickly find that it is certainly there in many forms—

from watches and class rings to the finest cultured pearls. In fact, it may be difficult for you to draw the line at exactly which jewelry is okay to take and which would be better left at home. Your child is certainly going to have some strong opinions, depending on what he is used to wearing and what he sees his classmates wearing.

At the very least, good jewelry should be locked away when it is not in use. A roommate may be completely trustworthy, but unlocked dorm rooms, other students, or even visitors from other schools make security a real issue on campus (see Chapter 6).

CHECK your homeowner's insurance. Are your student's belongings covered while he is at college? You may need a rider to your policy, especially for any jewelry brought to school.

BED AND BATH

"When the sheets looked dirty on one side, he turned them over and used the other side."

"My son spruced up the room for Parents' Weekend. I had never seen a T-shirt used as a pillowcase."

Your child may be used to shopping for his own clothes, but he may be less familiar with, or even uninterested in, all the bed and bath items he will need. You may choose to purchase everything new or use what you have. You may even receive offers in the mail to rent linens from a service on or near campus. (Before agreeing to any of these, check the quality.) Whatever you decide, here are the essentials. (See Appendix A for checklist.)

- Sheets. Two or three sets of *extra-long twin* will be sufficient. Don't buy flannel unless you are sure that the climate at school and in the room will call for it.
- Mattress pad. The thicker the better.
- Pillows. Besides bed pillows, your student might also use throw pillows or a bed rest if he works propped up in bed—but, again, don't buy what your child is not accustomed to using.

- Pillowcases. Include some extras. If your child doesn't change the entire bed, a clean pillowcase is a good compromise.
- Comforter. You may want to add a duvet cover to protect the comforter itself from too much wear and tear.
- Blanket. Know the climate your student will be living in, and don't buy the wrong weight blanket. It can be layered with the comforter in the coldest weather and need not be heavy enough to stand on its own. Lighter-weight blankets also come in handy in very warm dorm rooms.
- Towels. Supply your child with three to six bath-size towels and a few hand towels and washcloths for quick washups. Wet towels don't dry on the floor (where they are often left), but dorm rooms may not have enough space to hang too many large towels.
- Shower caddy and toiletries. Toothpaste, tooth brush, shampoo, soap dish, shaving equipment, etc. can't be stored in dorm bathrooms—they have to be carried from the room.
- Sundries. You may want to wait until you get to campus to purchase supplies. Don't buy giant sizes that will be too heavy and won't fit in the caddy.

A Word About Laundry

The classic picture of the child lugging home bags bulging with dirty laundry may indeed come true at some point during his college career—but it is also true that he will have to take care of the laundry by himself on a more-or-less regular basis. The campus is likely to have coin-operated washers and dryers (sometimes within the dormitory), and it may even include a centrally located laundry service of its own. If the campus is in or near a town/city, commercial laundry facilities will be readily available.

With all of these options, how students do laundry—and when—will depend to some extent on their schedule and the patterns of roommates and friends. Don't assume that a "messy" child will never get out the box of detergent, but don't expect first-year students to change sheets and wash socks on a weekly basis. Be sure your child understands which clothes can be machine washed and which must be dry cleaned. Go over the basics of separating by color! However your student chooses to do the laundry, *don't forget to pack a couple of laundry bags.*

Although it is tempting to sign up with a commercial service (on- or off-campus) merely to assure a standard close to that of home, think about it first—particularly before paying in advance:

- Where will your child have to take the laundry, and how will he get there? Is there pickup and delivery? Will he use it on a regular basis if there is not?
- What percentage of the students use the service? Your child may not want to do what very few, if any, of his friends do.
- What is the reputation of the service? The student grapevine will be active, and negative reports will discourage all but the boldest (or most desperate).
- Can you quit the service and get a refund if your student decides to do his own laundry?

Even if your student does his own wash, investigate a reliable cleaning source so that you have a ready solution when he calls, bogged down in work and out of clean socks. Many laundromats provide a wash-and-fold service for a fee.

ALL THE OTHER STUFF

"He was surprised when the lights went out in the dorm. I wasn't, because in my son's room alone there was a microwave, a mini refrigerator, two tape decks, two computers, lamps, clocks, and fans."

"It was 100 degrees in the shade on move-in day. The first thing we did was to plug in the fan—in the one electrical outlet in the room."

The number of electrical gadgets and gear your student will enjoy at school is limited only by his budget and the electrical capacity of his dorm. Check the college regulations before purchasing any equipment, and have your student coordinate who's bringing what with his roommate. (See Appendix A for checklist.)

- **Extension cords, power strips, and electrical converters.** Most dorms will not have enough outlets, and the ones they have may be the old-fashioned two-pronged ones.
- Small appliances. Some students bring (or rent) small refrigerators and microwave ovens to keep and prepare snacks and even meals. Don't lug a heavy refrigerator, however, without looking into renting one on or near campus—the nominal charge may be worth the alternatives of hauling it back and forth or finding storage. Students may also use popcorn poppers, hot pots, and coffeemakers. (But many colleges prohibit microwaves, hot pots, and the like. Check first.)
- Fans. Most dorms are not air-conditioned, so fans can be a lifesaver in warmer climates.
- Musical equipment. Students may prefer to bring their own CD player (or tape deck) even if their roommate has one. Earphones, with long cords, are helpful.
- Video equipment. Depending on the size of the room, students bring small televisions, VCRs, or video-game equipment.
- Athletic equipment. Again, dorm room space is usually at a premium, but if your child is interested in sports, be sure he packs the appropriate equipment (for examples, tennis racquet, golf clubs, free weights). Many colleges have intramural programs so that even the weekend athlete can play.

Telephone and Answering Machine

Almost all college dorms are wired for telephone service, but you will probably have to pay a hookup fee. Most schools require students to bring their own handsets. (Buy an extra-long cord to permit ease of movement.) You may want to consider a cordless phone that permits the student to walk around the room, sit at a desk, or even walk into the hall for privacy. *One drawback to these phones*—they're easily "lifted" by visitors and should not be left lying around in an unlocked room.

Check to see whether your student will need an answering machine or if the college provides, for a fee, voice mail as part of the telephone service.

Computers Are Another Story

Does your child need a computer, or would a word processor do the job? Certain majors (engineering, architecture) and some colleges require every student to buy a computer, often a specific model. It's probably wise to include the cost of a personal computer when figuring any college budget.

Although most schools advise students that there are computers on campus available for use, check out the number, the location and its security, and the hours they can be used. Will your child be comfortable and safe in the computer center if he is working on a paper in the middle of the night? How real an option will this be for your student? Relying on the campus computer center—or computers belonging to friends—may be difficult before major paper deadlines.

Another plus for owning your own computer is the local area network so many colleges now use to connect your student via his PC to the school library and other campus facilities. This will facilitate any required research. Finally, many colleges belong to Internet, an international computer network (a major part of the "information highway"). Students, using their own PCs, can tap into off-campus data banks and libraries. As an added bonus, Internet permits students to communicate via E-mail with other students as well as with teachers on their campus and at other schools. Note, however, that all dorms are not hooked up for network capability, and students on some campuses must rely on central computer facilities.

When purchasing a printer for the computer, consider size, speed, and noise level. Bubble-jet printers are much more compact than dot-matrix versions. Given that there must be room for the keyboard, the monitor, possibly the central processing unit, and a printer (not to mention books, notebooks, a lamp, etc.) size does count. Furthermore, will your student want to print a paper on a noisy machine if his roommate is asleep in the next bed?

If you or your child already own a computer, decide whether you want to pack that one up for his use at college. He may prefer the comfort of a familiar machine and software. Before packing the computer for transport, be sure the hard drive is "parked."

If you plan to buy a new computer, you may decide to wait and purchase one at school. Most colleges offer significant discounts on machines, so the difference in cost, even compared to a discount store at home, may be negligible. More important, many schools offer service only on those machines they sell. Computers purchased at school will definitely be compatible with the college network.

TIP: Do not discard computer boxes—you'll need them for packing at the end of the year.

One drawback to buying the computer on campus may be the availability of specific machines. One student, who ordered her computer when she arrived on campus, had to wait two months before it was delivered. In the meantime, her English professor required weekly papers. The student ended up using computers of other dorm residents, working at their convenience, not necessarily hers.

If you plan to buy a computer from the college's service, consider placing your order during the summer, rather than waiting to arrive on campus. If you are unfamiliar with the models offered in the flyer or catalog from the computer center, visit a local computer store to actually *see* the products. When one student saw the dimensions of one of the printers she had considered, she changed to a smaller model because of limited dorm desk space.

Before making any decision, check with the campus computer center to determine what system and software is most commonly used.

INTERIOR DESIGN

"My California student created his own beach in his room—complete with palm tree and sand. When we arrived for Parents'

Weekend, we looked up to see strands of lights blinking around the window."

"The suitcase was almost closed when my daughter realized that she wanted to take something else along—us. We all lined up for a family picture."

Beyond the necessities of clothes and linens, the contents of the dorm room will be limited only by school regulations, size, arrangements with roommates, and your child's own imagination. Before he plans anything too elaborate, review any printed do's and don'ts from the college. There will be a housing contract to sign that spells out student responsibility for the room.

REMEMBER: If your student has a roommate, be sure the two of them discuss any major decorating decisions.

In any case, it's probably wise to see the actual dorm room before committing to any large-ticket or unusual items.

Most colleges provide a bed, desk, closet, and bureau or built-in storage. Some also include a lamp and a wastebasket. The rest is up to you. Here is a list of basic items most students will want to have. (See Appendix A for checklist.) Your child may want to wait and buy some of these items imprinted with the college logo.

- Lamp. Even if the college provides one, it will usually not be bright enough for much studying. Your student may also need a separate lamp for reading in bed—perhaps one that he can clip onto the headboard or nearby bookshelf, desk, or windowsill. If the lamp your child takes with him requires hard-to-find bulbs, be sure to include some extras.
- Carpet. If the room does not come with one, most students find it easier to buy one after they get to campus when they see the exact size of the room. Upperclassmen often hold informal "yard" sales of rugs and other decorating items in the college quad during the opening days of school—bargains abound.
- Storage units. Small cubes will hold desk items; larger stacking boxes will store clothes or extra towels and can also serve as a table. (The trunk that was used to ship things from home will also have this dual function.)

- Alarm clock. As loud as you can find—two would be a blessing for a heavy sleeper.
- Wall hangings. Mirrors, posters, calendars, bulletin boards—all bear a very personal stamp and distinguish one room from another.
- Pictures/albums. Photographs of family and friends, as well as high school yearbooks, help bridge the gap between life at home and life on his own.

CARS ON CAMPUS

"Hi, Mom; don't worry. I just filed the police report. They'll try to find the car."

"My son called to tell us that he'd gotten a terrific internship in town, 15 miles from campus, but he still hadn't figured out how to get there on time."

Having a car on campus is a privilege and a responsibility. As many families will admit, the privilege belongs to the student, while a great deal of the legal and financial responsibility stays at home with the parent. Taking a car to school means that your student will have to assume much of the day-to-day responsibility for maintenance, as well as to deal with real—or perceived—pressure to serve as the campus chauffeur. Even worse, students may be tempted to lend the car to others, a bad move for a myriad of reasons. Safety and parking concerns are additional worries. As a result, many colleges discourage first-year students from having cars at school; some even prohibit them.

On the other hand, having a car at college can be a real advantage. There is no question that on many sprawling campuses a car would help reduce student wear-and-tear in the mad dash for classes. Furthermore, many schools now participate in consortiums with neighboring colleges, permitting students to take classes at other campuses. While shuttle bus service is generally available, hours may be limited or shuttle stops may be at a distance from the dorms. Having a car can reduce transportation costs from home to school and back again. (However, it also becomes much easier to take "road trips" to visit friends on distant campuses.)

REMEMBER: You will no longer control where or when your child uses the car.

Parking

Before taking a car to campus, be sure your student considers the available parking. Most colleges strictly enforce no-parking zones, and tickets with escalating penalty fees are freely distributed by campus police. Besides the cost of registering a car on campus and any parking charges, consider:

- How far is parking from the student's dorm? Is there shuttle service?
- How secure is the parking lot—for the car *and* the driver?
- What is the rate of car theft on campus (ask the college security force or the local police)?
- If the campus is located in the snow belt, will the car need covered parking and how quickly is the parking lot plowed?

Insurance

Notify your insurance carrier when your student takes a car to school. Your premiums will probably change depending on the college's location (an urban campus may push your rates higher, while a suburban or rural campus could lower them). If your child has a good driving *and* academic record, your rates may also be reduced. Before he leaves, be sure he:

- is familiar with the insurance coverage you have;
- knows the name and phone number of who to contact in case of a claim, and has accident report forms in the glove compartment;
- has the car registration and insurance ID card with him. **TIP: Keep a copy of them yourself.**

Getting the Car to Campus

If you live at a distance from the school, you may not want your child driving the car that far. Consider using an insured-car carrier service. Check with several moving companies about how they transport vehicles for families that are moving. A reputable service will be completely insured and will give you a firm pickup and delivery date for the car. The cost will depend on how far away the school is, whether you drive to a depot or have the car picked up from your home, and whether you have it delivered directly to campus or to a depot nearby.

Don't plan to load the car with boxes before shipping it unless you check the insurance coverage of the carrier—the contents of the car may not be insured against theft.

Maintenance and Service

Finding a reputable repair person is the responsibility of the student while the car is at school. With the expense this might entail, it's a good idea to have the car completely serviced before it leaves home. Have your student speak to the family mechanic about routine maintenance that should be done while the car is on campus. A road service, offered by many companies, might also be helpful as added insurance in case of emergency. If you already have such a service, be sure it extends across state lines.

A Word of Warning

Caution your student that having a car on campus has to be a selfish venture, one to share with friends only when he is behind the wheel. A casual trip to the airport or nearby mall with someone else driving your car could result in an accident or injury that can be an insurance—and friendship—nightmare. **THE GOLDEN RULE OF CAMPUS CARS: Never lend a car to a friend.**

BAG IT: PACKING, STUFFING, AND SENDING

"My son figured it wouldn't take any time at all. He would just pack the suitcase he used for vacations, and off he would go."

"She kept insisting that she wanted to take a bean-bag chair to college. I finally told her it was either the chair or her mother in the car—we couldn't fit both."

Before plunging into the business of packing, think about how and where you want to pack everything. Whether you do it all at once or a little at a time, plan ahead so that you don't make the mistake of putting too many heavy things in one box—after all, who will carry it?! Follow these guidelines:

LABEL EVERYTHING

1. Clearly identify every box, suitcase, duffle bag, etc.

2. If a dorm room has been assigned, include that number on the label. It is your student's new address and will bring misguided luggage directly to him.

3. Mark what is in each container to speed up unpacking.

4. Keep an inventory of what your student is taking or shipping to college in case of loss or theft.

Soft-sided, collapsible, duffle-style luggage or extra-strength *clear* trash bags make ideal gear for bulk items like clothes and bedding. These containers can be emptied and collapsed, take up very little space, and can be easily stored for the trip home. Cardboard boxes can be used to transport or ship items and then broken down for recycling after move-in day.

One ingenious freshman packed her clothing in colorful storage crates inside boxes so that when she arrived on campus, unpacking and stacking her crates instantly organized her wardrobe. You might also think about using a larger, wardrobe-style box with a clothes bar (a moving company will have it)—your child's clothes will go from his closet to the box to the dorm closet, already on hangers.

Dressier clothes can also be packed in a trunk, along with more fragile items like lamps. The trunk can then be turned into a "table" for the room and can also store seldom-used (or out-of-season) items. Unless you have the original container for delicate electronic equipment, contact the place of purchase for advice on how to pack it safely—or contact a local moving company for suggestions.

REMEMBER: When items are unpacked, containers must be stored or disposed of!

If your child is planning to send a bicycle to school, check out the shipping requirements, unless it will be going by car. An already assembled bike may not be accepted, and there may be size limitations as well. An airline will take a bike for a set fee plus a charge for a box or bag. If this is your plan, arrive early so that there is time for airline personnel to ready the bicycle for the trip.

Getting It There

When the campus is close enough to reach by car, it's just a matter of stuffing everything into the available space. When the distance is too great for driving, you have several options for getting your child's belongings there.

If you are flying, most airlines allow each passenger two checked pieces, one carry-on, and an additional piece, either luggage or a box, for which a fee is charged. Because these large duffles or boxes can weigh as much as 70 pounds, this might prove to be a sound option. (Check with individual carriers.)

REMEMBER: When you arrive, all of this luggage must be transported to campus. Reserve a large rental car, station wagon, or van in advance.

You may instead choose to have everything shipped to campus. Check out the packing/mailing services offered by the U.S. Postal Service, United Parcel Service, Federal Express, D.H.L., Airborne, local mailing services, local and long-distance movers. The prices and options offered by each can vary widely.

Before sending anything, read the scheduling material sent by the school, as well as the instructions for deliveries to campus. Be sure your child will be available to receive packages on the given day (or that someone else can do it for him), and verify exactly where they are to be delivered. If you can coordinate your student's arrival on campus with items shipped from home, arrange for two-day delivery. Schedule pickup for the day before he leaves for school, with delivery set for the day after he arrives. Just to be on the safe side, have him carry basic linens and several days' worth of clothing.

TIP: LABEL, INSURE, AND TRACK PACKAGES.
College offices are prepared for most eventualities and will usually help a student locate an errant box or trunk. Make duplicate copies of all receipts so that the student takes one list with him to school, while the other remains safely at home. Keep all receipts until the items arrive safely on campus.

Most commercial carriers suggest that clothing, bedding, and bulky unbreakable items be shipped by surface, while electronic gear (stereos, computers, televisions) be shipped overnight or second-day delivery to cut down on handling of these items.

OTHER OPTIONS

1. Send items to a friend or relative in a town near campus.

2. Ship (with permission) to a satellite office of your employer or to the hotel/motel where you will be staying.

3. Send ahead of time to college storage facility.

It took years to create a comfortable home environment for your child—and that's really what you are trying to *recreate* at college for him. You want to focus on what works for your child—what clothes make him comfortable? What purchases will ease his transition to school? These lists are suggestions— what has worked for many kids, but not necessarily yours. You'll probably have to modify or add to the list once he is at school and sees what is popular on campus.

YOU CAN BANK ON IT | 2

"My daughter worked during the summers while she was in high school. Even though she used part of her earnings for birthday gifts, movies, going out, and so on, we had always chipped in when she needed something extra. Before she went to college, we deposited what we thought was a semester's worth of money for her expenses and figured she would use some of her own money, too. After two weeks at school she called home, crying that she had already spent all the money we'd given her. Her own savings were still intact."

Money is more than dollars and cents, and college is more than what is learned in the classroom. By the time your child graduates, you hope that he has a plan for the future *and* the life skills to accomplish his goals. Learning how to budget money, pay bills, handle a credit card responsibly, balance a checkbook, even choose and use an Automated Teller Machine (ATM) are all part of College 101. From the age of 18, your child will be starting his own credit history. Making sure that it's a clean record is also part of his education.

But how money is dealt with can have deep psychological ramifications for parent and child. Growth into adulthood is a continuing process of separation. But it's hard to be completely independent while still tied to your parents financially. Many kids, although thankful for the monetary support, resent the continuing dependence and the emotional baggage—real and imagined—that it brings.

It's also tough for parents, at times, not to use their financial clout to try to correct behavior or channel their college student in a certain direction. Some parents threaten to withdraw monetary support if their child doesn't pursue a particular academic program or achieve a certain grade ("I don't pay for Cs"). Ideally, parents should never use money to influence behavior, but the temptation to do so may become strong and in some situations difficult to resist.

By the time your child is ready for college, you should include him in the planning of how you will pay for his schooling and discuss what his financial contributions, if any, need to be. Then help him develop a reasonable budget for his living expenses, and determine how your own budget at home is going to be affected by his absence. No matter where your student will be, the availability of money and how to gain and control access to it should be prime concerns. This entire process is another, and very important, affirmation of your belief in his maturity. It demonstrates your confidence in his ability to handle money.

PAYING THE BILL

"My daughter called in tears—my ex-husband hadn't paid the tuition, and she was going to be barred from classes."

"The way I figure it, I'll be retired and still making payments on all the loans I've taken out to put my kids through college."

The deposit you send to hold your student's place in his freshman class is but a drop in the bucket. Now you'll have to pay the rest of the bill, which will include amounts for tuition, room and board, and student services. If your child has received a financial aid package from the school (consisting of scholarships or grants, loans, and/or work/study), the amount left for you to pay may still be sizable. Even if you don't qualify for need-based aid, you may want to look at different options for dealing with the cost.

NOTE: If you're divorced or separated, be clear about who is responsible for payment—it is your child who will be barred from classes if it is not received. Whatever the terms of the settlement, the responsible party may not always live up to the agreement. If you foresee a problem, contact the college financial aid office. Don't wait for the last minute.

Payment Plans

Generally, colleges issue bills before each term for tuition, fees, and room and board. Unless you make other arrangements, the bill will be mailed to your student at his home address. Credits for financial aid (scholarships, grants, monetary awards, loans) are subtracted from the fixed charges. Miscellaneous charges for things ranging from library fees to parking tickets will be billed monthly and are payable upon receipt. If your student has overlooked a charge during the year, it may appear on a separate invoice during the summer. One parent was annoyed when he discovered that the $15 parking ticket his son had ignored first semester had now doubled.

TIP: If you have any question about the bill, contact the bursar's office or the financial aid office before sending in your check. Get the name of the individual who helped you for future reference.

Paying what you owe before each term is the most direct way of handling the bill. There are other methods of payment, however, and as the parent of a college student, you'll be receiving information about them from the school as well as from outside agencies.

One possibility is to enroll in a monthly payment plan for a small annual fee. Plans like this can stretch your payment out over the course of the school year. They don't involve borrowing or interest charges and can be used to supplement other aid or financing options.

Another option available is the Insured Tuition Payment Plan in which you make regular payments to an outside agency. You'll begin by making 8 or 10 monthly payments (eventually 12 payments after the first year), thus lowering your monthly outlay. Again, you pay a small fee when you apply, but there is no interest; in fact, your payments during the months your child is not in school earn interest for you at money-market rates while the plan is in effect. You receive the interest earnings when the plan ends. Depending on what state you live in, this plan also provides insurance coverage that will make the remaining college payments in case of your death or total disability.

If your financial circumstances permit, you may be able to take advantage of an option offered by some schools—a Tuition Prepayment Plan. By prepaying four years of undergraduate tuition, you lock in the rate that is in effect during the year your child is a freshman, avoid future tuition increases, and have the security of knowing that you've taken care of all the tuition bills. Note, however, that this doesn't cover increases for fees and room and board, nor does it come cheaply, as some quick arithmetic will tell you. Check the agreement form carefully to see how the college will deal with refunds, study abroad, leaves of absence, accelerated study, or withdrawal from school. If you're going to prepay tuition by liquidating assets, you should weigh the savings in tuition increases against the loss in investment income. If you're going to borrow to make the payment, find out first whether and how you can deduct the interest expenses.

What About Loans?

College expenses may be more than you can handle out of your current income or savings. Loans taken out by you or your child can help make up the difference.

Your student may apply for a Federal Stafford Loan, a low-interest loan with a repayment period of up to ten years. Remember, though, that the longer that interest payments are stretched out, the higher the *total* amount you pay. Higher payments per month result in lower overall cost. Depending on the student's financial need, interest payments may be subsidized by the federal government while he is in school and for six months afterward. If there is no such need, or if the subsidized amount is not enough to cover his costs, he can take out an unsubsidized loan, but he'll have to pay the interest monthly while in college or have it accrue adding to the principal that he'll repay after graduation. The total amount available through a Stafford Loan is capped, however, and may still not be sufficient to meet your needs.

Passage of the Federal Student Loan Overhaul Program set the stage for schools to lend money directly to students—without going through banks or other private lenders. This program has an extended payment option, but again the longer the repayment period, the higher the total cost. Check with the school's financial aid office to see whether your student's institution participates in the plan.

Regardless of your income, you might look into long-term financing through loan programs such as the Federal PLUS Loan or the SHARE Loan. These would be parent or family loans, and repayment of principal and interest must begin while the student is in school. Although you don't have to demonstrate financial need, you may have to undergo a standard credit check. If you don't qualify, your child may still be eligible for additional funds from the unsubsidized Federal Stafford Loan program. Any of these loans will allow you to borrow the full net cost of education, including personal and travel expenses, after deducting any other form of financial aid.

TIP: Contact the college to find out whether it has a preferential loan plan that is better than a national one.

Things to consider when you decide to seek a loan:

- Assess your credit history. If you haven't been regularly employed, or if you already have a large mortgage, home equity loan, car loan, and so on, you may not be eligible unless you have a credit-worthy coapplicant.
- Determine which loan program will meet your full need.
- Decide whether you prefer fixed- or variable-rate financing.
- Note the repayment period—will it conflict with any future financial needs (educating younger siblings, for example)? Is there a prepayment penalty? (There is none for the two specified above.) Will you be able to meet the monthly repayments in the future?
- Compare the interest rates and fees.

- Analyze your current budget—which monthly payments are feasible for you? What is the maximum you can afford to pay monthly?
- Select one plan and apply on time. If you're applying for the maximum amount (full cost minus financial aid and other grants or loans), you can only file one loan application at a time. When you learn how much—if anything— you can get from that source, you can reapply elsewhere.

NOTE: If your child has applied for financial aid from the college, the amount of that aid (if any) must be determined before any outside loan application can be processed.

Taking Out Insurance

Suppose your student has to lose a term because of illness or injury. Although the college may return tuition/fees if he withdraws near the beginning, there's a sliding scale of repayment as the term goes on. If you can't afford to lose what you've paid (and then make an additional payment when your child is ready to return), find out whether the college offers a Tuition Refund Plan you can subscribe to.

Earning Expense Money

The cost of a college education has been compared to housing and feeding your child for four years in a hotel at a distance from your home. The size of the bill may mean that he'll have to (or want to) work while he's at school, either to help pay the school bill, to earn his own expense money, or to be as independent as possible. Some parents even feel that learning how to earn money is part of a college education, and recent studies suggest that work experience during college helps secure a job after graduation. The number of hours a student chooses to work will be an individual decision, but the fact of working is an increasingly common phenomenon.

The campus employment office and job bulletin board are good places to start the employment search, and if there is a shopping mall nearby, it can also be a source. The availability of jobs may be dependent on campus location, with perhaps fewer options in rural areas. Before committing to a position, however, the student should be sure that he can handle the hours required, that the location is a safe one (particularly if he'll be there at night), and that he has a way of getting there if it's at a distance from campus.

Keep in mind that working in a clothing or bookstore can bring welcome discounts, that eating while on a restaurant job can save on the food bill, and that ushering in a theater saves the price of a ticket. If your child is going to deliver food to campus or elsewhere, find out whose vehicle will be used—and be sure your car insurance covers him. Students with the proper certification can sometimes find work as lifeguards at local pools.

Beyond formal employment, your child may create his own job as tutor, party aide, baby-sitter or house-sitter (usually for local faculty). If he has a car on campus, he may even drive people to the airport. Some students do laundry for a fee or print T- shirts with clever logos to sell (check college rules first). Some type their classmates' papers for a fee. Remember, too, that volunteer work can lead to paying jobs.

Some Points about Financial Aid and Work/Study Programs

If you've filed a financial aid form, your child may receive part of his money by working on campus. These jobs pay minimum wage or higher (directly to the student), and they offer the advantage of flexible hours linked to the school calendar, as well as a way of involving a student in the school. Check with the financial aid office about the different kinds of opportunities available.

TIP: There can be a three-week lag in salary payment, so be sure your child has enough money to cover the beginning of the semester.

If your child is eligible for financial aid, you'll be required to fill out the federal forms each year, whether or not your financial circumstances have changed. Don't forget to get your tax return in order early—applications for the second year can be filed after January 1. Remember: Just as when you first applied, 50 percent of your child's W-2 earnings and 35 percent of his assets will be counted toward the amount your family is expected to contribute to the cost of his education.

If Your Financial Situation Changes

Anything can happen—and frequently does—between the time your child is accepted to college and the end of his freshman year. If you're on the receiving end of a financial bonanza, it'll certainly make all those bills easier to digest. If, on the other hand, fate intervenes and deals a financial blow, college expenses may seem impossible to bear.

This is the time to be completely honest with your child. He may not have been planning to work during the school year—now he may have to. You may no longer be eligible for the parental loan that was going to pay for tuition—he may have to apply for a student loan. The money available for trips home, entertainment, and so forth, may have to be drastically reduced. In the worst-case scenario, he may even have to transfer to a less expensive school or commute to one closer to home.

Open communication between you and your child is important in order to avoid resentments that can spring up on both sides. A parent who loses his job has to deal with his own loss of self-esteem—as well as the anger of the child who sees his college dreams shatter. You and your student may not have the same priorities in a financially changed situation, but you can both benefit from an honest discussion about it. You may be surprised by what he is willing to give up, just as he will appreciate being taken into your confidence.

As far as the college is concerned, notify the bursar's office immediately when you are unable to meet a scheduled payment date. Many schools will make arrangements for payment extensions.

Whether or not you are already receiving an aid package, contact the financial aid office. An existing package can be adjusted to fit the changed circumstances. If you didn't apply or your application was denied, you might now be in a position to receive some eleventh-hour financial help.

REMEMBER: Financial aid packages and outside loans for sophomore year are based on tax information from the preceding calendar year.

When the financial emergency occurs after January 1 of freshman year, be sure the financial aid office is aware of those circumstances when your application for sophomore year is processed.

BUDGETING

"We have just begun to come out of our own personal recession." (Parent of a recent college graduate)
"I finished shopping—and my grocery cart seemed empty."

Developing a reasonable budget—and learning to live within it—are the goals for you and your child. Of course, that first semester you may under- or overestimate the amount of money that will be needed. But constant overdrafts or end-of-the-month shortages are a sign of trouble.

Separating out the big ticket items, such as tuition and room and board, you and your child need to discuss other living expenses. You'll have to decide:

- Who will supply the spending money—you, your child, or both?
- If you're giving him money, will you make deposits monthly or provide a lump sum for the semester or year?
- What will you do if he runs out of money?

Budget Guidelines for Campus

For many students, budgets happen only after a big mistake. But the ability to develop and stick to a financial plan is an important part of the financial education you hope to give your child. Budgets for freshman year, however, necessarily have to have some flexibility. Despite your best estimates, there are some hidden costs, such as extra dollars needed for dorm room furnishings and decorations (some of which the student can use for the rest of his college stay) and the cost of learning from money mistakes as your student develops sensible spending patterns.

Generally, budget between $100 and $300 each month for spending money, depending on the location of the college campus and the available student activities. Regular expenses will include:

- Laundry and dry cleaning
- Toiletries
- Haircuts
- Phone bills
- School supplies
- Snack food and eating out
- Newspapers and magazines
- Postage and stationery
- Recreation

Encourage your child to budget for these but to save a portion of his money for the "extras" he's going to want: additional clothes, school-logo items, CDs and tapes, and gifts. The student who has a car needs money for gas, parking, and a student-parking permit. Fraternity and sorority members have dues to pay. Beyond this, you may want to pad the budget a little for the first term to include higher-than-usual telephone bills (to home and high school friends) and perhaps additional trips home or to visit friends on other campuses. Halfway through the year, you'll want to review with your student his financial situation and decide if he needs any adjustment for the rest of the year. It's a good idea to encourage him to keep $100 in reserve for emergencies. He might lose a contact lens or a pair of glasses. Bikes break down, and sneakers disappear.

The Budget at Home

You invest a great deal more than love in the child who goes off to college—it's an expense that may have affected your bank balance for a long time already, and it's certainly going to impact your life now, no matter how you pay the bill. If you're making monthly tuition payments, that extra debit has to be squeezed in beside the mortgage or rent, telephone, electric, heating, etc. Paying by the semester may affect vacation plans and even how much you spend on eating out or family celebrations. If you've already put aside the money for your child's college, you will still see adjustments to your budget at home in terms of the money you don't spend regularly on your child's food and the amount you now start paying for your own trips back and forth to campus, long-distance phone bills, and the initial "start-up" expense of outfitting him for campus.

Whatever your financial position, it's important to be honest with your child:

- Let him know how much you can afford, and then allow him to determine how he allocates the expense money you give him.
- If he's counting on you to pay bills or make deposits, be sure you meet the deadlines.
- Make him aware of how much it's still costing for the siblings at home—everyone's needs have to be balanced.

Once your family has determined how much money you will contribute for expenses, your next question becomes how your student gains access to it.

CHECKING ACCOUNTS

"It took me two days to straighten out his checking account. I never knew the kid ate so much pizza. He had at least a dozen checks, each for $10, made out to the pizza delivery boy. Then when I finally balanced the account, the next month he bounced three checks again."

"He never bounced any checks, but I almost went crazy when I helped him balance his account. He constantly wrote checks out of sequence."

Does your child need a checking account? It's one way for him to access funds and pay bills—but it also gives him leeway to access more than is there! One student merrily went on writing checks, without ever noting the amounts in his records. He relied on the ATM to give him his current balance, not realizing that uncashed checks could alter his financial picture drastically.

Before deciding how to set up the checking account, ask yourself how well your child handles money:

- Can he stay within his allowance?
- Has he had part-time jobs?

- Has he been responsible with his own money?
- Has he paid any of his own expenses?
- Has he ever had his own checking account?
- Is he organized enough to reconcile the monthly statements?

Once you've made a realistic assessment of your student's financial savvy, you're ready to answer two fundamental banking questions:

- Do you open a joint checking account or one in his name only?
- Is the account at your hometown bank or at a bank near campus?

Why Choose a Joint Account?

If your student has little experience with money, a joint account will give you legal access to information about account balances, as well as the opportunity to deposit additional funds before there is an actual shortage or bounced check. If the account is set up with a savings account linked to checking, you'll also have legal authority to transfer money quickly from one to the other. Even with joint accounts, checks can still be imprinted with only the student's name and address.

REMEMBER: It's easy for an inexperienced—or harried—student to forget to enter in checking account charges or withdrawals from automated teller machines.

Monthly statements can be sent to the school or home address, but if your child is a novice at this, the latter might be a better option. You'll be reconciling the statements while he's away, but he can take over the responsibility when he's home.

Why Choose a Separate Account?

The student who is paying all of his own expenses or who has already handled financial matters responsibly would do well with his own checking account. If he doesn't already have one, it might be a good idea to establish the account the summer before freshman year so that he has time to learn the mechanics of balancing a checking account. Then he's on his own. With this option, you're supporting your child's ability to take charge of his own financial life.

Whichever type of account you choose, be sure to ask about a provision for preventing overdrafts. Banks have different names for this service, such as "cash reserve" and "checking plus," but it is built-in insurance that will cover any shortage in the checking account. The student will not be writing bad checks. Generally, there is no charge for the service unless it is activated by an overdraft. The student should be aware that these floating cash reserves carry high interest charges when used and that overdrafts and service costs must be repaid.

Your next decision is where to open the account: in your hometown? near the campus? or both?

Why Choose a Hometown Bank?

An account in a bank in the student's hometown will give him a consistent base and ease transactions when school is not in session. If you choose this course, however, call the college ahead of time to find out the policy in that area for cashing out-of- town checks with college identification. Some areas are more lenient than others, particularly college towns used to seeing drivers' licenses and other out-of-town identification. As a rule, students can cash out-of-state checks at the student credit union, but the hours and dollar limits at these school facilities may be restricted. Bank location doesn't matter when checks are only used to pay bills by mail.

If you're not going to have access to the account, check with your hometown bank to see whether it permits electronic fund transfers by telephone or even via computer hookup. If your bank doesn't have this electronic capability, it may allow the student to put on file a letter authorizing the bank to transfer money from a savings account to checking in case of an over-draft or if an emergency occurs.

Why Choose a Bank Near Campus?

You may prefer to open an account near the college. If your child is going to be working while at school or receiving other checks, having a local bank will make depositing them much simpler than mailing the checks back home, and funds will be available for use much faster. You may also find that some colleges have established special relationships with local banks that will give students certain concessions such as lower minimum-balance requirements and/or free checking.

The disadvantage of having the account near campus is the additional mailing time it takes for parents to deposit checks into the account. One parent solved the problem by mailing postdated checks to her son well in advance of when he needed to deposit them. Remember that out-of-state checks take five to seven days to clear unless you've made arrangements with the bank to waive this requirement.

If you've chosen a bank near campus, develop a contingency plan for emergencies where large sums of cash might be needed. If you want to wire money through your bank at home, you must do it during banking hours. Check the times, days, and fees for this service. It will take 24 hours for the funds to be available, so money wired on Friday may not be in your child's hands until Monday due to federal banking regulations. If you use a commercial service, the fees will be higher, but the hours may be more flexible and the funds available sooner.

The account at the bank near campus also brings with it the extra hassle of depositing checks by mail if your child will be home during the summer. For those families, it might make sense to have an account in both places, perhaps a savings account at home for summer earnings and a checking account at school for deposits and expenses there.

TIP: Check out the minimum balance and service fees before deciding how much to keep where.

Establish a Personal Relationship

Wherever you open an account, try to establish a personal relationship with a banker. Always get the name, title, and phone number of a contact. If you decide to keep the account in the student's hometown, set up an appointment for him with a banker who will explain the rules and requirements of checking and savings accounts. The banker also becomes the student's contact. Similarly, the bank near campus is used to

---

BANKING TIPS

1. Develop a budget *before* college starts.

2. If you'll be contributing to expenses, decide whether you will deposit funds by the month or by the semester.

3. If your child will be using his own earnings, advise him to hold some money in another account instead of making it all available at the beginning.

4. Call the college before making your decision about a bank. Find out the names of banks near campus and which one(s) have a relationship with the school and are well regarded in terms of courtesy and hours by students.

5. Set up the near-campus account *before* you go there by sending for the forms and doing the paperwork by mail. Otherwise, get to the bank early to avoid the long lines during the opening days of school.

6. Your student doesn't need hundreds of checks and might be better off with only one book at a time.

7. If your child is going to have a checking account for the first time, teach him before school starts how to maintain and balance his checkbook.

8. Caution him to store checks in a safe place that he will remember.

9. In the event that you need to wire your child money, you'll need to know his bank's ABA code and his account number.

---

dealing with students and will be able to explain how the accounts work. It is not uncommon for these bankers to warn students about impending fund shortages.

Good banking relationships may also help save you money. For example, when one student spent a semester abroad, her mother asked that the monthly fees be waived for that time period. Establishing a personal contact with a banker in the branch near campus during freshman year helped expedite the request.

AUTOMATED TELLER MACHINES (ATMs)

"The ATM machines were constantly running out of money. The trick was to make your withdrawal before six o'clock on Friday night. Otherwise you could end up going all over town looking for a machine that had some money for the weekend."

"You mean you have to deduct the ATM withdrawals from your checking account?"

Most banks will automatically issue a bank card that can be used to access cash, and they have become as much a part of daily life as checks. Money is literally at your fingertips within moments, often when there's no place open to cash a check. If your child hasn't had unlimited access to the handy plastic card before now, it's certainly going to change the way he thinks about—and handles—money. Even if he's been using one already, it may still be tempting to feel like the proverbial kid in the candy store without a parent hovering nearby.

These machines, however, aren't always reliable; some may run dry at times, break down, or otherwise be out of order at the most inconvenient times. One student spent an hour one Friday afternoon, searching for a machine that was not out of cash. Especially on weekends and holidays, ATMs often run short.

Just as parents need backup systems for dealing with cash emergencies, students should also be prepared. Help your child develop a list of alternate ATMs that are safe and convenient to campus. Encourage him to get cash early so that if the ATM isn't available, the bank or student credit union is still open.

Because bank cards are the simplest way to access money, the ATM system may influence your choice of which bank to use. Some are strictly local or regional, while others, like CIRRUS, are nationwide. Check with the college to find out what systems are available on and near campus and how each system accesses cash. For example, some bank cards don't work on money-market accounts outside the home state. If you haven't set up the right type of account, your child won't be able to withdraw money.

Transaction fees will differ among banks and even within the same bank depending on the type of account. Some banks offer a limited number of free withdrawals per month; others charge not only for each withdrawal, but also for using an ATM to check balances; still others may have no fee.

REMEMBER: Stress caution and safety over convenient location. Some machines may not be in a secure area for nighttime use.

USING THE ATM

If your child will be getting his cash from an ATM, remind him to:

1. Record an ATM withdrawal in the checkbook; it's the same as writing a check or making a cash withdrawal from a bank's teller window.

2. Keep the bank card in a safe place, and never give it to anyone else to use.

3. Choose a PIN number that's easy to remember (but not the first four digits of his Social Security number or telephone number), and never disclose it to others. Keep a record of the number at home in case he forgets it!

4. Check the safety of ATM locations. They should be well lit, in a safe area, and well patrolled by campus or area police (when in doubt, ask a friend to go along).

CREDIT CARDS

"I gave my son a credit card on my account when he left for college. Two weeks later, I went to charge some tickets, and my card was refused. My son had charged his books and some meals on the card, and I was at my credit limit."

"The first month my daughter was at college, I got a bill from VISA for $800 worth of CDs. I paid the bill, but she spent the next two years paying me back."

Charge! In a sense, the word is still a battle cry, but now the trenches are college campuses, where credit cards may be too easy to come by, and even perhaps the home front—unless there's a clear understanding of who's paying the bills.

A credit card is certainly convenient, obviates the need for carrying large sums of cash, and may be accepted where personal checks are not. In the hands of the wise, it can be used to plan the following month's expenses; in the hands of the foolish, it can drain a bank account.

If your child is going to have a credit card at school, you have two options: put him on your account with an authorized user card, or have him apply for his own credit card with its own credit line. When he's on your card, the only legal restriction on the amount he charges is the limit of the credit line. One parent opened a monthly statement to discover that the student had charged airline tickets to fly his girlfriend to campus for the weekend. Another parent was embarrassed in a store when a salesperson declined her credit card because it was "over the limit."

Obviously, you need to discuss with your child when and how much he can use your card. Don't forget to tell him to write a check (or forego the expense) if you are close to the limit and have a purchase of your own to make.

The advantage of having the student on your credit card is the higher credit line it carries. Large purchases such as books, which can total more than $500 per semester, or even airline tickets home may exceed the credit limit on a student card, which can be as low as $300.

If you decide that your student should have his own credit-card account, remember that parents don't have access to the card and can't look at the balance in the account.

REMEMBER: These cards will help establish the student's own credit history, but they can also damage a credit rating if payments are not made on time.

Although the credit line on a student account will start out lower than that of the parents, thus limiting spending ability to some extent, it can still be a sizable amount of money, depending on the bank. Furthermore, a good payment history will generally lead to automatic increases in the credit line. One parent discovered to her chagrin that her daughter's limit grew to exceed hers after the student paid small monthly bills in total and on time.

Another possibility is to combine both options so that your student has your credit line for big-ticket items and his own credit card for personal expenses. Decide before school begins who will pay which bills.

Be sure to discuss the options before your child actually leaves home and comes across restaurants and other public places offering brochures for student credit cards. There will probably also be opportunities to sign up for one when you get to the campus, and you might find that these cards have some advantages in terms of lower credit lines or interest rates.

It's easy (perhaps too easy) for students to apply for and receive these cards. A current, validated ID from a four-year college or university along with a dorm address and phone number is often sufficient. For some of these cards, there are no minimum income or cosigner requirements; a summer job is an acceptable source of income, along with a bank account of some kind. As a parent, you may not even know that your student now has a VISA or MasterCard.

In some states, you may be asked to guarantee payment even though the card is in the student's name and it is his credit history. Even if you're not required to cosign, some states may hold you legally responsible for bills if you claim the student as a dependent on your tax return.

If you put your child on your credit card, the monthly statement will obviously be sent to you. Even if he has his own credit card, the bills can still come to you if he uses the home address rather than his address at college. Decide how much and when he will reimburse you for any of his bills that you pay.

As with a checking account, using the home address makes life easier when the student is not away at school. There will be no change of address during the summer or if he lives in a different dorm from year to year. *You* will be paying the bill but establishing *his* credit history until he can do it himself. If you do this, however, you'll see the charges, so the student obviously loses some of the privacy he may crave.

Credit-Card Debt

Unfortunately, credit cards are so available and convenient to use that students may abuse them. Some campuses even have credit counselors to help those saddled with debt they don't

CREDIT-CARD STRATEGIES

Whichever option you choose, teach your student some basic credit-card strategies.

1. Keep the card in a safe place. Report a lost or stolen card immediately. Be sure that both of you know the account number and the number to call.

2. Keep track of how much you spend. Set a budget for yourself ahead of time and don't exceed it.

3. Keep all receipts and check them against the monthly statement for accuracy.

4. Pay your bills in full and on time. Even if monthly bills state a "minimum payment," paying only that "minimum" will trigger a hefty finance charge.

5. Don't use a cash advance for one card to pay off another card.

6. If you can't pay the total bill, pay the minimum required and put the credit card away until you've paid the balance.

7. Avoid using a credit card to get "instant cash." Cash advances carry high interest rates from the day you get the money, whether you get it at a bank or through an ATM; there are no "grace periods" for cash advances, as is often the case with regular purchases.

know how to handle. All too often, students graduate with a bad credit rating and, in a worst-case scenario, land in bankruptcy court.

Your child may be enticed by offers of free airfare, gas, or clothing and sign up for not one but several cards (with or without your knowledge). If he does that, he multiplies the amount he can charge each month—but also the amount he is responsible for paying. What seems reasonable for one card quickly becomes overwhelming.

Be honest with your child before he even gets to campus, and teach him to use credit wisely. If you're not going to cover his bills, tell him ahead of time, but also warn him of the credit history repercussions when the bill is not paid. As a parent, however, it's going to be hard to turn aside the telephone plea for help, a fact that helps account for the low incidence of payment delinquency among students.

NOTE: Credit counselors see many instances of parents going into debt just to cover up their children's debt.

Other Accounts

Your child may already have joined clubs offering CDs, books, videos, etc. If he hasn't, he will certainly be exposed to mail-in offers when he's at school. When he first signs up, he'll get his choice of a specified number for free, but then he'll have to either pay for or return the selection of the month. At home, you were there to make sure that he did one or the other; at school, it's his responsibility. How easy will it be for him to mail back what he doesn't want? Is he the one who has been doing this at home? These bills can add up quickly, and failure to pay doesn't stop the monthly deliveries. Remind your child that this is also part of his credit history.

As your child becomes ever more familiar with money and how to manage it, the questions and rules will change. What works for your freshman student may not be appropriate for a more mature college senior.

What doesn't change are the central objectives of this whole process:

- Good communication of needs and expectations
- Avoidance of easy pitfalls and unpleasant surprises. How he deals with money should not distract him from his studies or strain the parent-child relationship.
- Affirmation of the growing independence and responsibility of a young adult who can handle basic financial decision making.

IN SICKNESS AND IN HEALTH | 3

"It was six weeks into freshman year. We got a call at 11 o'clock at night from our son—he was in the emergency room at the hospital near campus. He'd been fooling around with some other students—seeing who could slam-dunk a doorjamb! He jumped and slam-dunked his head instead! Like most head wounds, it bled all over the place. The resident advisor took him to the hospital. The cut on his head took six stitches, but on the phone he complained that his ankle hurt from where he landed when he fell. We suggested that he mention the pain to the doctor before leaving the hospital. Turns out he'd broken his ankle and was in a cast for the rest of the semester."

Dormitory life seems to breed disease, and freshmen are particularly susceptible to every germ and virus lurking in the halls. And why not? Heady with the first flush of college life, students stay up late, eat poorly, and live in rooms that are frequently either too hot or too cold. It's almost like nursery school when your child was introduced to a group experience and seemed to catch one cold after another. Injuries, from accidents (often related to alcohol abuse) or from just a bunch of schoolkids fooling around, are also common.

It's tempting to diagnose and offer advice over the phone to your child who is complaining about "feeling rotten," but like everything else about college, this too should be a learning experience. Perhaps for the first time, a student will have to deal with illness on his own. He will have to recognize when he is getting sick and know what to do before it is serious enough to call you for advice. There may even be emergencies when he will have to obtain appropriate treatment, often without your input.

But this is frequently difficult for first-year students. Just like adults, they may be reluctant to go to a new doctor for help. Your child may feel shy or modest. Some young men who have never been seen by a female doctor may encounter one through the campus health plan; a young woman seeking birth-control information may be embarrassed or worried that the information will be shared with her parents (it won't). Your student may not know how to describe his symptoms adequately; he may even fail to recognize dangerous symptoms.

On the other end of the phone line, you may feel anxious if your child delays going to the health center or says that he is treating himself (based on expert advice from his roommate). You worry when your student claims that he "doesn't have time to see a doctor," or that he's heard "bad things" about the campus health service. Here are some things to consider:

- What health care is readily available to your child on his campus, and how sophisticated is it?
- What should you do if your child does see a doctor and the treatment seems inadequate or inappropriate?
- What should you do if your child is seriously ill? Should you go to campus or should you insist that he come home?

CONFIDENTIALLY SPEAKING

"Don't worry, Mom. There weren't a lot of stitches, and the bruise is almost gone."

"I called his dorm one night only to be told by his roommate that he was in the infirmary. It turned out that he had been there for three days."

A month after school began, a freshman called home, his voice almost unrecognizable—he had just had four wisdom teeth pulled and was looking for sympathy. He was supposed to have had the dental work done at home over Thanksgiving break, but on his own, he had decided he didn't want to ruin his vacation. **REMEMBER: Although you are paying the bills, if your child is over 18, you are entitled to none of the information about the medical treatment he receives.**

As much as colleges encourage students to share information with parents, laws forbid health services from discussing your child's case with you unless he gives his permission. This means that your child could be hospitalized and even undergo surgery without your knowledge.

How much medical news your student shares with you—and when—is up to him. Be sure he understands the concept of patient confidentiality so that he does not put off seeking medical care because he worries about your reaction to what is bothering him. Campus health providers cite alcohol use (and abuse), as well as sexual problems (rape, pregnancy, sexually transmitted diseases, etc.) as major sources of medical trouble and emergencies for students on campus. Your child may be hesitant to share this information with you. Reassure him that *all* information at the health center is confidential and that even if he is embarrassed about talking to you, he must be honest with the health provider.

Despite the freedom your student will have, encourage him to keep you as fully informed as possible without infringing on his newly developing independence. If he agrees, give your home phone number to his roommate or dorm advisor in case of an emergency.

CHOOSING HEALTH INSURANCE FOR YOUR STUDENT

"Dad, is that little health card we use at home good for hospitals here?"

"My son was hospitalized for pneumonia during his first semester at college. Our health network told us that once he left the hospital, they wouldn't cover his follow-up doctor appointments unless we brought him home."

While a student health center can provide treatment for most common illnesses, you will still need health insurance for your college student to protect against injuries or illnesses that require emergency-room care, hospitalization, surgery, or outside specialists. You can choose to provide coverage under your family health insurance (most plans will cover full-time undergraduate students under the age of 24), or you can purchase a separate policy. Many colleges offer insurance plans for students and will include the cost in term bills.

REMEMBER: If you opt not to carry the college plan, be sure to deduct the cost from your tuition bill.

In deciding which option to take, compare the plans and determine:

- Will the student have the same benefits at the same cost under your family plan when he is away at school?
- How will claims be filed, and by whom? If you have to do the filing, your student will have to notify you about any medical treatments or absorb the cost on his own. The student will have to weigh confidentiality versus cost.
- Does your family plan require participants to see specific doctors? Is there an affiliated group near campus? How will he get to the doctors if he doesn't have a car?
- Does your family policy require participants to use specific, preapproved hospitals? Is the hospital most likely to be used by the college for emergencies on your network's list?

Health Network Insurance Plans

If your family is enrolled in a health network, coverage for your college student may become more complicated. Discuss your options with a company representative. Some plans permit your student to transfer to an affiliated network near campus. (If you do this, however, check to see how coverage will be handled when he is home for breaks.) Other plans insist that the student remain in your local network, regardless of the distance from campus. Many require you to call an emergency "hot line" number to receive permission to see a doctor other than your primary care physician. Most plans will cover any emergency treatment or hospitalization at in-network rates, but the question of who will treat your child for follow-up care differs from plan to plan.

If You Choose the College Insurance Plan

In reviewing the college insurance plan, you will want to know:

- Does it give better coverage than your family plan, and will it be in effect when your student is home or away from school?
- Does it cover care given only by specific physicians affiliated with the college? Will your student be able to use referrals from home and still be covered?

You may decide to carry double coverage for your student, continuing to cover him under your health plan and electing the college health insurance as well. This is a more expensive choice, but paperwork will be reduced at your end, and you will have the assurance that all situations will be covered. It is also another way of giving your student responsibility for a major part of his life—his health care.

REMEMBER: If you elect to carry the college insurance, if he is 18, the student receives his own policy and does not have to tell you when he files a claim even if you pay the bill.

PREVENTIVE MEDICINE

"The cold winter in Boston triggered asthma in my southern California daughter, but she thought it was just another New England cold—until she was rushed to the emergency room with a life-threatening attack."

"It wasn't until we had to complete the medical forms for college that I realized that my son had never received a second measles shot."

Before your child ever arrives on campus, he will fill out a medical history form and get a physical from his primary care physician at home. Use this opportunity to bring all records up to date and complete any care that may have been neglected or put off.

Although forms may differ from one college to another, they will probably ask for a record of immunizations, any known allergies, chronic conditions, and past hospitalizations.

Note which immunizations are required by state law and which additional ones are recommended. For example, hepatitis B may not be required, but many health providers strongly suggest the series of three shots as a precautionary measure. Plan ahead for this because there is a minimum waiting time between the shots. You may also want to update his tetanus vaccination (recommended, but not yet required at most colleges).

Dental and Vision Care

While colleges require physical exams, your student should also be checked by his dentist and an eye doctor:

- At a precollege visit, have X rays taken to spot trouble that might be brewing.
- Know ahead of time what dental care is available on campus. What if emergency oral surgery or orthodonture work is required?
- If your student wears a retainer (or braces), be sure the fit is correct before he leaves home. He should have his hometown orthodontist's phone number with him in case the appliance is lost or broken.
- If your student wears glasses or contact lenses, he should have a copy of his prescription. If financially feasible, keep a spare pair of lenses and/or glasses on campus.
- Make provision for emergency replacement of glasses or contact lenses. Is there an optician near campus who can fill his individual prescription (some are more difficult than others), and is there transportation available?
- Keep a copy of the prescription at home as well, in case the student loses his copy or cannot get it filled as quickly as you can.

Allergy Alert

You may want to check with the campus health center about allergies common to the area, especially if your child is prone to allergies or hay fever. Find out when the allergy season is, how long it is, and which sensitivities are affected. If your child receives regular allergy injections, be sure his physician at home knows where the college is; the frequency or strength of injections might be affected. Arrange to bring the necessary supply of vaccine with you to campus along with a current written prescription. Find out ahead of time where the vaccine will be stored and how your student should arrange to have his injections.

REMEMBER: Your child may not need shots for an allergy condition in his hometown, but living on campus may aggravate the allergies he already has (or may create new ones).

Be sure he knows how to recognize allergy symptoms so that he doesn't just suffer along, thinking he has a cold. The health center can provide information, if not treatment, for the new condition. Asthmatics should know how their illness will impact activities at school, how to recognize an oncoming attack, and what to do about it.

Chronic Conditions

If your child is receiving treatment for a chronic condition or is undergoing physical therapy, talk to the provider at home about how to continue treatment on campus. Ask whether your student needs to be under medical supervision or whether he is at the point that he can continue a program on his own. Don't forget to have him bring appropriate prescriptions if he is going to continue supervised treatment on campus. If he cannot receive the necessary treatment at the school's health facility, find out where he has to go, and decide how he will get there on a regular basis.

Talking to the Doctor

This may be the first time that your student has had to take responsibility for his health. To familiarize him with the process, have him make and keep his own appointments with doctors and dentists the summer before college. He should ask his primary care physician if there is any information about his health history that the college health center and any attending physician should know.

Discuss with your child the information a doctor needs to make a diagnosis:

- A description of obvious symptoms and how long he has had them
- Changes in the symptoms
- Similar illness he has had previously
- Chronic diseases he may have
- All medication (including vitamins) he may be taking

The student should also tell the physician about any sensitivities he may have to medications and be very clear about whatever prescription he receives:

- What kind of medication is it and what is it for?
- What is the dosage?
- Will there be side effects? (If it causes drowsiness, what should he do about an upcoming test or paper?)
- How long should the medicine be taken?
- Should there be a follow-up visit?
- What is the name and phone number of the person who provides the service in case of further questions?
- Are there any contraindications? For example, alcohol and some medications can be a lethal mix.

Pack a First Aid Kit

Besides any regular medications your child normally takes, include in a first aid kit: antiseptic salve; nonprescription antidiarrhea medication (discuss with your child proper dosage), aspirin or nonaspirin pain reliever, and bandages. You may also want to pack sunblock, a thermometer, and over-the-counter cold medication (again discuss proper dosage and when to see a doctor).

MEDICINE 101

Before your child goes off to school, think about the medical information you use in dealing with your own family. The more knowledge he has, the better off he will be.

1.   Does your student know to ask for a plastic surgeon when stitches are required for his face? Your student should understand that he has up to 24 hours before the facial wound must be stitched. This should allow him enough time to find a good plastic surgeon.

2.   Burns, from hot pots and microwave ovens, are common. Does your student know to put cold water on the burn as quickly as possible? Does he know to leave blisters alone—don't open them with a needle?

3.   When playing sports, working out, or after a fall: soreness is one thing, but swelling means that something is wrong. Use the RICE treatment until you can see a doctor—**R**est, **I**ce, **C**ompression (ace bandage), and **E**levation.

4.   Cold symptoms that last more than two weeks could signal something more serious—see a doctor.

5.   Never take a pill that has been prescribed for someone else.

Mono Alert

Mononucleosis is a real problem on campus. For most patients it's a mild disease, but if contracted when papers are due or around exam time, it can wreak havoc on a student's studies. Although it is not as easily transmitted as other ailments such as a stomach virus, it is a communicable disease. The problem is that unlike a stomach virus, which lasts 48 hours, this disease can incapacitate the student for weeks. The symptoms are: slight fever, chills, swollen glands, sore throat, and fatigue.

College students are at special risk of contracting mononucleosis because they are living in close quarters and are frequently run-down from lack of sleep. Even if your child is not showing any symptoms, advise him to be tested for the disease if one of his friends or a roommate comes down with mono. Students must see a doctor for further evaluation.

Treatment for the disease consists primarily of resting and waiting for the blood count, liver, and spleen to return to normal. In acute cases, the doctor may prescribe steroids. The patient must avoid any contact sports or intense physical workout for at least two months to avoid rupturing his spleen. He must not resume any strenuous physical activity until the doctor approves and must not take aspirin.

Most campus health services will permit students with mono to remain on campus either in their dorm rooms or in a medical facility, depending on the severity of the case. If you believe that your student's case is lasting more than a few weeks or that his health care is not being closely supervised, you should bring him home or insist that he get another medical opinion.

TALKING FRANKLY ABOUT SEX

"Sex under the influence of alcohol is not any kind of sex I want."
"I spend most of my time counseling girls when they come to me with pregnancy scares."

Sex on campus is an issue that parents worry about and students discuss among themselves. While over the years most parents have had many conversations with their children about sex, it's especially important to bring up the topic again before your child leaves for college. While students undoubtedly think they already know everything there is to know about the subject, this discussion will in fact be different. It's less about mechanics and more about values, health dangers, concerns, and pressures. You should offer advice rather than dictums and extend the perspective of age rather than rules.

The reality is that men and women may have their first sexual experience in college, many as freshmen. Your student will have to confront situations and decide for himself what he wants to do—but hopefully with as much knowledge as possible.

NOTE: Even if you know, or suspect, that your child is already sexually active, in this day of AIDS, you need to have a frank talk about sex before he leaves for school.

Why the Concern?

The freedom enjoyed by college students is heady. As universities have abdicated their role as *in loco parentis*, it's up to students to decide how to handle this flush of independence. They are now making decisions we, as parents, used to make for them. Here's why many parents worry:

- Despite laws prohibiting the sale of alcohol to anyone under 21, beer and hard liquor are generally readily available and prevalent.
- Parties can and do get out of hand.
- Peer pressure can be intense.
- Young adulthood is the age of experimentation, and students may become sexually active before they are emotionally ready.
- Parents may have strong moral or religious beliefs that forbid premarital sex.
- Living on campus is like living in a fishbowl. Relationships frequently develop at a faster pace because you can be with someone literally 24 hours a day.
- Birth control devices are available at most health centers; no parental permission is required.
- Most schools don't have curfews or restrictions on visitors and overnight guests of the opposite sex.
- Dorms are coed.

Is Everyone Doing It?

At freshman orientation at a large, liberal eastern university, a senior counselor led the discussion on sex on campus. While he admitted that many students were sexually active, he also discussed his decision to remain a virgin. It's not as uncommon as you would think.

But if peer pressure in high school was intense, it can be even more so on a college campus. What parents need to make clear to their student is that becoming sexually active needs to be a conscious decision, not a response to the fear of being the "oldest living virgin." If your student chooses *not* to pursue premarital sexual relationships, he may need reassurance and reinforcement in order to avoid feeling "socially isolated."

It's also important to talk frankly about your own moral values and opinions about premarital sex, recognizing that your children may not agree with any or all of your views.

NOTE: Moral issues aside, one message must be clear: because of the threat of AIDS, no one can afford to be promiscuous or reckless.

AIDS on Campus

As one campus health official described the situation, "College students are in a state of denial. They believe that AIDS can't happen to them." The teenage sense of immortality contributes to this dangerous misperception about the threat of AIDS. Rarely do students ask sexual partners to be tested for the disease prior to beginning a relationship.

REMEMBER: Parents must discuss the need to practice "safe sex" even if other forms of birth control are being used.

Even as you are making clear your own moral values about sex, it would be irresponsible not to discuss how to prevent AIDS. You may choose to preface the conversation with a plea for abstinence as the only sure method of not contracting the disease, but it's important to tell students to:

- Be sure sexual partners are honest about their previous sexual relationships.
- Insist that any sexual partner be tested for the HIV virus.
- Use a latex condom until both partners have been tested and found HIV-negative for six months.
- Avoid entering a sexual relationship unless both partners agree to be monogamous.

In addition to discussing AIDS in a sexual context, parents also need to caution students about transmission through contact with blood products or through infected needles. Professional and varsity college sports now require that any player who is bleeding immediately leave the field of play until the bleeding is under control. Students playing in pickup games and intramural sports must also insist on these rules. Similarly, advise your student to avoid sharing razors. While the chances of transmitting AIDS under these circumstances are extremely remote, it's a well-taken precaution.

Finally, while intravenous drug use on campus is not common, it's a danger that has to be discussed, especially in the context of AIDS. Sharing intravenous needles is a leading cause of AIDS transmission.

Sexually Transmitted Diseases

It's easy to forget, with the threat of AIDS, that there are other equally dangerous sexually transmitted diseases (STD) that can have long-term effects on your child's health and fertility. You need to stress to your student the need to practice safe sex, not only to avoid AIDS, but other sexually transmitted diseases as well. Even if a woman is using birth control pills, a condom is the only way to avoid STDs. Unfortunately, women suffering from an STD are also at higher risk of contracting AIDS.

Herpes, gonorrhea, chlamydia, syphilis, and venereal warts are still common, especially among young people who have multiple sex partners. Your student should not hesitate to seek medical treatment and must be honest with the doctor about his partners. For most STDs, treatment is successful and simple if started early in the course of the disease. There is concern, however, about the growing ineffectiveness of antibiotics because some STDs have developed strains resistant to previously effective antibiotics.

Birth Control Options

Most campus health centers will prescribe a method of birth control to their students. They will provide counseling and describe the options available. But before your daughter leaves for college, even if you would prefer that she abstain from sexual relationships, it's important to discuss any family health history that might impact on her choice of birth control. For example, a familial history of high blood pressure might preclude the use of birth control pills.

Similarly, it's critical that men understand the need to share the responsibility for birth control. Stress that partners must discuss clearly and frankly what birth control will be used *before* beginning any intimacy.

Students attending colleges that do not dispense birth control devices will need to go off campus in order to get protection. Again, whatever your own personal preferences, insist that your child get competent medical advice before beginning any sexual relationship. The local hospital, medical association, or Planned Parenthood can recommend an off-campus doctor.

BODY IMAGE

"My friends and I would go out for something to eat almost every night, even though we'd already eaten a full meal. My mother almost fell over when she saw me at Christmas. I'd gained 10 pounds."

"My roommate offered me some over-the-counter diet pills. I didn't realize how dangerous they could be."

Away from home and now responsible for their own eating habits, some students gain weight, some lose weight, and others, in response to the pressures and stress of college life, develop eating disorders. Still others, determined to reshape their body image, are tempted by a quick fix and use illegal steroids.

It's all too easy to put on the pounds. The "Freshman Fifteen," the extra weight that freshmen students gain during the first year of college, is a common complaint. Even those students who complain vigorously about dorm food find that bread, ice cream, and desserts are usually quite edible. Doughnuts replace healthy snacks or serve as breakfast; alcohol is readily available but is loaded with empty calories; and late-night pizza is a dormitory staple. Many students are no longer on an athletic team and don't make time for regular exercise in their busy schedules.

There are many reasons why parents should encourage students to maintain healthy eating habits and exercise regularly. Unsightly weight gain can affect a student's self-esteem. Furthermore, when a student is staying up late, partying hard, and not eating properly, he is more vulnerable to colds and other viruses.

If your student has gained unwanted pounds, caution him against crash diets or taking appetite-suppressant pills. Many students are lulled into thinking that if a drug is available without a prescription, it's safe. Whether it's an appetite suppressant or a cold pill, warn your child to read the fine print about possible side effects and contraindications before taking any medication.

Losing Weight Unintentionally

While some students are adding unwanted pounds, there are others who will come home painfully thin—not from an eating disorder, but because they hate the food, are too busy to eat, or a combination of both. Don't be overly concerned. Unless there is a real health danger or you suspect an eating disorder, vacation time at home generally restores most students to a healthy size. It also helps to send "healthy snack" Care packages as a gentle but direct suggestion.

Eating Disorders

Some health officials estimate that up to one-third of the women on college campuses suffer from some eating disorder. Anorexia (controlled starvation) and bulimia (a binge-and-purge syndrome) are the most common. These eating disorders are *not* nutritional problems but emotional ones that primarily affect women. Anorexia and bulimia frequently begin in early adolescence, and a student may have already undergone a successful treatment program. But symptoms may resurface in college.

If you suspect that your child is suffering from an eating disorder, insist on professional help. The problem cannot be handled alone. Many campuses have support groups for students like this. Your child may also need individual therapy, either with a private doctor or with college health professionals. If the campus health center doesn't have the facilities or staff to monitor your student's case, check with the nearest hospital or medical association for professionals who provide treatment. As a last resort, bring your child home to get help. Eating disorders can be life threatening.

Anabolic Steroid Abuse

Anabolic steroids are forms of illegal drugs that are present on campuses. Synthetic drugs that facilitate adding muscle bulk and strength, steroids can have dangerous, even potentially fatal, side effects. While frequently associated with athletes, steriods are abused by many students who use the drugs to improve their body image. Athletes are more likely to use steroids only for the length of the sports season, while body builders may abuse them on a more regular basis. Advise your student about the dangers of steroids, and caution him to refuse to use them even if they are suggested by a coach, trainer, or friend.

ALCOHOL AND DRUG ABUSE

"Last year at my school, two students died from an allergic reaction to alcohol."
"If you want drugs, you can always find them."

Keg parties are the legend and lore of college. Indeed, the trend on many campuses is to begin partying on Thursday. One recent study revealed that students spend $5.5 billion annually on alcohol, more than on nonalcoholic drinks and books combined. Almost every campus has tragic stories about accidents—even deaths—from alcoholic overdoses. While alcohol is the drug of choice on most campuses, marijuana, amphetamines, and other illegal substances can also be obtained generally by those who are in the market.

Whether or not your student chooses to use—or abuse—alcohol and drugs is a decision he will have to make. You can advise, suggest, and worry, but as with much of college life, the ultimate decision will be his.

But it's important for students to remember:

- Alcohol and drugs impair judgment.
- It's more difficult to recognize danger when under their influence.
- There is a strong correlation between substance abuse and serious accidents, date rape, and general ill-health.

Be Honest About Family Problems

Have a frank and honest discussion with your student about any alcohol-dependency problems within the family. These kinds of family secrets may mask a problem for your child. You must alert him to any genetic predisposition to alcoholism.

Beer and Wine Contain Alcohol, Too

Students sometimes treat beer and wine, especially fruity wine coolers, as if they were soft drinks, ignoring their alcoholic content. Alcohol is alcohol—the body does not distinguish between beer and whiskey.

REMEMBER: You can develop alcohol-dependency problems even if you drink only beer and wine or even if you only drink on weekends.

There Are No Quick Cures for Intoxication

While we would hope that our children never drink to excess, be sure your student understands that there is no easy way to sober up. The body has to detoxify itself and that takes time. Black coffee doesn't sober up a drunk—it only makes him more awake—nor do exercise, cold showers, or food help rid the body of alcohol. On the average, a person can metabolize about one drink (one beer *or* one glass of wine *or* one shot of liquor) per hour without getting drunk, but that is dependent on an individual's size, weight, and body metabolism.

What If His Roommate Has a Drinking Problem?

Despite the best of intentions, your student cannot be responsible for his roommate's or friend's drinking problems. You should advise him:

- Don't be an enabler. That means that it's not your child's job to make sure his roommate gets up for classes on days he has a hangover, or to share notes for missed classes, or to provide cover with the resident advisor, college authorities, or even the roommate's parents.

- Don't succumb to pressure to drink with him so that he feels more comfortable.
- Talk to the resident advisor if your roommate's drinking is impacting on *your* life. Think about asking for a room change if his drunkenness constantly disrupts study and sleep, because drunks make terrible roommates.

The Dangers of Alcohol

Students often don't realize that intoxication can be life threatening. If a friend or roommate has been drinking to excess, monitor his condition. Get help immediately (from a resident advisor, the campus health center, or the campus police) if:

- Breathing is very slow or irregular.
- The pulse is weak, very fast, or very slow.
- The person has passed out, is asleep, or can only be roused slightly for a few moments.
- The person's hands or feet are colder than normal.

SEEKING MENTAL HEALTH TREATMENT

"I was really worried about my daughter's emotional state. I knew she had been seeing a school psychologist, so I called him and tried to discuss my daughter's case. He refused to talk to me, citing confidentiality laws."

"My daughter didn't recognize the signs of bulimia until her roommate confessed that she had a problem."

The first year at college can be a pressure cooker. A student must learn to juggle academics with independent living. While the opening months at school are exciting, they're often scary as well. Meeting new people and making new friends without the security of a home base can throw some youngsters into a tailspin. Even for those who have gone to camp or lived away from home before, college life is different—and kids know it. The freedom can be heady and frightening.

Before leaving home, students should be reassured that emotional problems at this time are normal and that seeking help is wise, not necessarily an indication of something serious.

Colleges are prepared to cope with emotional and mental problems, and many have mental health professionals on staff. Frequently, students just need the reassurance that they are "okay." Your child might want to talk to his resident advisor, a member of the clergy, or a counselor at the campus health center. Short- term therapy, often a few sessions with a campus psychologist, can often put the student's problems in perspective.

Many schools have a myriad of peer-group counseling programs for problems ranging from eating disorders to procrastination. If groups are not available on campus, the school will have alternative plans for student treatment. By knowing ahead of time what facilities and staff are offered, you will be able to provide a distraught child with suggestions for care. Again, your student's treatment will be confidential unless he gives the therapist permission to discuss the case with you.

If your child has been in therapy at home, discuss with your local doctor how to handle continued care. Some doctors recommend that students come home on a regular basis for treatment; others will provide telephone consultations; still others will suggest a consultation with an on-campus therapist to set up long-term care.

ASSESSING HEALTH CARE ON—AND OFF—CAMPUS

"My son called and told us that the campus doctor had made a diagnosis of tuberculosis. Terrified, we brought him home. He only had a bad case of bronchitis."

"Hi, Mom. I'm waiting for my roommate to get back from class so she can drive me to the infirmary. I'm using paper towels to stop the blood."

How and where students receive medical care varies from one campus to another, depending on size and location. Familiarize yourself and your student with the services available on his campus. Be sure to note:

- What services are offered? How far is the health center from your child's dorm? If not within walking distance, how will he get there?

- What are the regular hours for routine care? Are appointments necessary?
- Where does the student go when the health center is closed?
- Are specialists available on campus? If not, how will your student get to them?
- What are the phone numbers he will be using to access care?
- What hospital does the college use?
- Is there an overnight campus infirmary?

Tour the student health center with your child when you visit the campus before enrollment or at least when you arrive in the fall. It will help put him at ease about using it. You can also take the opportunity to advise the center of any specific chronic conditions your student may have.

If your questions cannot be satisfactorily answered on campus, don't wait until prevention reaches emergency status; develop an alternate plan suitable for your child's needs.

- Use your primary care physician at home, as well as the eye doctors and dentists in your community, as sources for referrals near campus.
- If you know people living in the area, ask them for recommendations—don't forget about those you will meet through your student when he gets to the college. One East Coast mother of a West Coast student met a parent who lived near campus, and they exchanged phone numbers. The acquaintanceship paid off when her son needed emergency dental work in the middle of the night.
- Depending on how seriously ill your student is, you may want to go to campus or even bring him home for treatment. If there is distance involved, check with the airlines for emergency fare rates.
- When there are serious questions about a diagnosis, have your family physician call the college health service for a consultation. Your child should always get the name and phone number of the person who treats him.

A Note of Caution

Sometimes your child's own reluctance to go to a doctor or a less-than-satisfactory experience at the health center may color his opinion and even his willingness to use the campus facility. Before opting for an alternative, find out why he refuses to get treatment there. Is it the student grapevine? Should he have made an appointment instead of waiting on a long line? One student received only a cold pill for an illness that had gone on for two weeks—but he hadn't mentioned his history of allergies nor how long he had been sick.

Certainly there are situations that call for off-campus care, but check out the legitimacy of the complaint before you look for an alternative.

At first the idea of becoming responsible for his own health care may not mean very much to your child. After all, you have been there with the reminders, the cold syrup, and the information. The longer he is away, however, the more he must learn to rely on his own instincts and knowledge. To do this he will need:

- A solid base of information about his own personal health and about the new community he will be living in.
- An understanding of the patient-physician relationship and some knowledge of the expectations he should have as a health care consumer.

LIVING WITH STRANGERS: 4
AN ARRANGED MARRIAGE

"As we drove into campus, in a ten-year-old station wagon stuffed to the gills, I glanced in my rear-view mirror, and right behind me was a chauffeur-driven Rolls-Royce! Following the Rolls was a small van. We all pulled up in front of the same dorm, and a man in a suit and his son got out from the car each carrying a small duffle. Then two guys got out of the van and started to unload boxes and cartons. We all headed down the same hall and then stopped in front of the same door. My son and I looked at each other. I knew he was thinking the same thing I was—how was a kid from a poor family like ours going to get along with a millionaire? You know something funny—they roomed together all four years."

Imagine going on a business trip, arriving at the hotel, and being told you had to share a room with a complete stranger—for a year! Your college student is worried about many things, but high on the list is roommate compatibility. Will I like him—will he like me? Does he party a lot—or is he a bookworm? Does he go to sleep at nine—or does his evening just get started at midnight? What kind of music does he like—and at what decibel level? Is he neat—or a slob like me? Will we agree on smoking, drinking, politics, morality, ethics, friends, courses, etc.?

Whether or not your student has previously shared a room with a sibling, living with a college roommate is a different experience. It's generally not as hard an adjustment as might be expected, even for those who have never shared quarters. While most freshmen miss the privacy of home at some point during the year, most also genuinely enjoy the intimate company of other students who are also experiencing the excitement and pressures of college life for the first time. If college is more than the sum of the courses taken over four years, certainly one of the most important lessons is learning to live with others, discovering the differences and similarities of a wide range of people, respecting the give-and-take of relationships, and developing deep and lasting friendships that come from sharing space with people who were once strangers.

It's a delicate balancing act: Colleges are trying to match roommates' interests, while at the same time encourage diversity. How successfully housing directors accomplish their task can make a noticeable difference for your child. If it's a good fit, a roommate can be a lifesaver in a sea of strangers; if not, freshman year can be more difficult.

THE HOUSING CONTRACT

"My son couldn't register for classes until he paid the bursar bill for his broken dorm window."

"At the end of the year, when my daughter took down posters from her dorm room, she had to spackle the holes in the wall—otherwise there would have been an additional charge."

Sometime before he actually moves in, your child will receive a list of housing regulations and be asked to sign a contract. Be sure he reads it carefully and understands that he is liable for what happens to the physical condition of the room. Besides any obvious or immediate problem, like a broken window, college maintenance may "sweep" through the dorms during winter break or wait until the end of the year to make any necessary repairs. At some schools, the cost is absorbed by house dues paid by the entire dorm; other colleges will bill your child directly. The latter will automatically divide the cost of repairing the damage without assessing responsibility unless one roommate comes forward and takes the blame. Any serious damage or vandalism could appear on a student's permanent record. One senior discovered that a freshman prank that resulted in a broken dorm window was still on his record and could have affected his application for a graduate-school loan.

Although the bill for the room is directed to the student, you may in fact be the one paying and can arrange to have any bills mailed home. In any case, your child is held responsible for seeing that the school receives the money. If you foresee a problem about paying a bill or question the validity of a charge, talk it over honestly with your child, and be sure to contact the bursar's office for guidance (see Chapter 2). Administrators note that all too often a student is caught in the middle, with the college on one side asking for payment and parents on the other withholding it, either for lack of funds or because they are challenging a charge.

REMEMBER: The student, not the parent, signs the housing contract with the college and is the contracted individual.

HOME SWEET HOME

"I encouraged my son to apply for a single room in his freshman year. He's easily distracted, and I thought the extra quiet time would help."

"My daughter, who'd always had her own room, was worried about sharing space at college. Boy, were we surprised when we walked into her dorm room and discovered it wasn't a double, but a quad—with two sets of bunk beds!"

When your child selected his college, he made basic decisions about where he wanted to live for the next four years (urban or rural area, climate, section of the country) and about the size of the student body (large or small school). College admissions counselors tout the advantages of all-freshmen dorms (campuses or quads) or of multiyear housing, if their school uses one or the other exclusively.

Residential living has most certainly changed in the last 25 years. Some parents may remember a kinder, gentler dorm life that included maid service and bed checks. Now, the specter of coed living by dorm, floor, or hall might come as a surprise to many first-time parents. Unfortunately, your child may have no choice in that matter. One parent took her daughter to school and found out that the dorm voted by hall on whether to have coed or single-sex bathrooms.

Living arrangements vary from school to school and even from dorm to dorm within a given school. Your child may receive a housing questionnaire that gives him some options, but even if he has no choice, you will find that there are advantages as well as disadvantages to most situations.

"Do You Want a Single Room?"

Whether or not to have a roommate(s) may seem like an easy question to answer, but encourage your child not to make a quick response based only on his present experience or "horror stories" heard from friends in college. A younger sibling who coexists in a room at home may not reflect what life would be like with a first-year student of his own age. A child who has never had to share quarters may have a preference rooted in his home life, but the reality of college will most likely be different from what he has known.

The advantage of a single room is that the student will not be distracted by the presence of a roommate. He can maintain his own study habits, sleep patterns, and lifestyle without ever having to consider the wishes of someone else. There will be no arguments about music or overnight guests.

The disadvantage of a single room is that a quiet child may not be absorbed into campus life and friendships easily. If he is not planning to join an activity or play a sport in the beginning of the year, he may feel lonely and isolated, particularly if this is his first time away from home. Even if he is more outgoing, one argument for sharing quarters is that it's a learning experience in itself. Having a roommate forces your student to go outside himself, to compromise, to share.

Don't force your child to select a single room for academic reasons without serious discussion about it first. Unless this is his decision, there is no guarantee that the absence of a roommate will help his grades. You will not be there to monitor his activity.

On the other hand, if your child wants a single room, don't pressure him to have a roommate. He is the one who has to live with the decision.

Before your child opts for a single room, check with the college about availability:

- Based on previous years, are there enough singles for first-year students who request them?
- If your child requests but does not get a single, what happens to him? Does he get a regulation-size double, or does he become the third one in an expanded double?

Coed Dorms

Very few schools, if any, had coed dorms in the "olden days" when parents went to college. But universities have found that residential life is enriched when men and women share space. There is less emphasis on viewing the opposite sex as potential mates and more attention to developing intellectual and platonic friendships.

No college permits men and women to live in the same dorm room. Some schools have coed floors with men and women living in separate but adjacent rooms. Other colleges place men and women on alternate floors. In some schools, bathrooms are coed with individuals expected to respect the privacy of other residents and knock before entering.

Is it one big orgy? Absolutely not. Residents tend to develop familial relationships, more like siblings than lovers, with dormmates.

Single-Sex Dorms

Although many freshmen will tell you that their college experience was that much richer because of all the new "brother-and-sister" relationships they formed, some students may elect to live in single-sex dorms. If your child likes the location of one of these (consult a campus map) and wants to develop a built-in network of male or female friends, this is something to consider. Some students feel that these dorms give them more privacy, as well as a place where they are not always "on stage."

As a parent, you should realize that this kind of dorm in itself does not preclude the presence of the opposite sex. Although the bathrooms won't be coed, that doesn't translate into no visitors to student rooms.

Academic Dorms

When your child is accepted into some colleges, he may have the opportunity to apply for a particular academic program that determines his living arrangements. If the program is truly optional for his college goals, be sure that he considers the dorm situation along with the course load.

- Is the dorm exclusively for those in the program?
- Will he be rooming only with other program participants?
- What are the opportunities for meeting first-year students not in the program?

While these dorms make it easier to work on joint projects, share material, and study together, they may also restrict the number of other students your child has a chance to meet.

Quiet Dorms

Offered as an increasingly attractive option at some colleges, these dorms have "noise curfews": no music, TV, parties, and so on past a specified hour. There will usually be only one dorm like this, although some schools are adding more because they have become so popular. Freshman dorms seem to be noisier than housing for upperclassmen, but each class—and campus—is different. Again, firsthand inspection before enrollment is probably the best guide.

Multiage Dorms

At some schools, your child will not have a choice about whether he lives with all freshmen or a mix of freshmen and upperclassmen. In other places, however, your child's decision to live in a theme or "interest" dorm (organized around everything from "quiet" to "athletics," "language" to "community service") may mean that he will be put with a cross-section of ages by floor or even by hall.

While his roommate will probably be a freshman, the first-year student who lives in a multiage dorm will have the experience and advice of upperclassmen, as well as access to a wide circle of schoolwide friends. The child who is easily distracted may well benefit because noise (even in "nonquiet" dorms) will usually be less. There is a natural tendency for students to pay more attention to academics and to become more serious as college goes on. As the mother of one student put it, her son had the best of both worlds—if he wanted to party at 2 A.M., he could go to where his freshmen friends lived; if he had a paper to do, he stayed in his own dorm.

On the other hand, a multiage dorm can be an isolating experience, particularly for someone who does not already know many first-year students and has no other way of meeting them. This problem may be magnified on a large campus. As a parent, you will also find it much more difficult to touch base with a cross-section of freshmen parents either when your child moves in or on Parents' Weekend.

If your child is interested in one of these dorms, or if the school has only multiage dorms, ask the resident advisor staff what efforts are made to bring the entire freshman class together. Of course, there is no substitute for on-the-spot observation: advise your child to look at the various living possibilities if he visits the campus after he is accepted. It will be as important to his happiness as is his satisfaction with the academic programs.

Substance-Free Dorms

In order to live in a substance-free dorm, a student pledges to refrain totally from smoking, drinking, and using illegal drugs. On some campuses, this pledge applies only to activity within the building where he lives (and he may not return there under the influence). This type of housing is attractive to those students who not only plan to avoid using these substances personally, but who prefer not to be around those who regularly indulge. Some student affairs officials also believe that this kind of residence may help students who are recovering from substance abuse. But the choice of this type of dorm must be a *personal* decision. If a parent insists on this housing over the wishes of his child, it is unfair to the other residents as well as potentially counterproductive.

ARRANGING THE MARRIAGE

"My son was afraid that if he told them how messy he really was, he'd get a roommate who was worse than he was."

"When I visited for Parents' Weekend, I heard loud heavy metal music coming from my daughter's room—I wondered whether her taste had changed. It turned out to be her roommate's stereo, but my daughter didn't seem to mind."

In the midst of all the other forms that arrive for completion, the one asking your child questions about his living habits probably draws the most interest—and concern—from him. The length of the form will depend on the college, as will the specific items. While some schools will give a detailed personality quiz, others will pose only a few questions. Most, however, will want to know:

- Smoking or nonsmoking?
- How neat are you?
- Do you listen to music while you study? What kind?
- How late do you stay up? Are you an early riser?

In any case, there are two major questions: How honest should you be? Does the form matter?

Your child is concerned about the impact of some of his answers. If he puts down that he keeps late hours because he studies at night, what will happen when he gets a roommate who likes to party all night? What will it be like to live with someone who is as messy as he is? If he smokes but doesn't plan to smoke in his room, should he put down nonsmoking? One freshman admitted that he lied on his form because while he knew he'd be smoking, he didn't want a roommate who did—he thought it would make the room too "smelly."

Although some schools have less sophisticated techniques for matching roommates, many use computers to create profiles of students based on answers to the questionnaire. It may also be true, however, that not all students return the form. Additionally, there are some colleges that pay little attention to them. Colleges must also consider meeting students' health needs and matching residents with other campus residential options. In any event, there will usually be a disclaimer to the effect that although every effort will be made to assign rooms based on preference, there is no guarantee.

From an administrator's point of view, a "perfect" match is rare, and sometimes there may even be a more positive living arrangement when the roommates are different. Although the housing office may not tell you how much weight it gives to the questionnaire, advise your child to be as honest as possible according to standards common to 18-year-olds, not adults. A "messy" room in your house may seem less of a disaster if placed side by side with his friends' rooms. His late hours may be more regular than the hours kept by someone who has to worry about making an early train in the morning. Realize, too, that behavior will likely be different in the new environment.

TIP: Resist the temptation to look over your child's shoulder as he fills out the form.

His answers may not be the same as yours would be, or even what you would like. Then again, you would probably not want to live in his room at home either.

One more caveat: No matter how well matched the roommates might be, you can't take into account who will be in the rooms on either side. One student who despised heavy-metal music found himself placed with a very compatible roommate, but on either side of their dorm room lived members of heavy-metal bands.

"Should I Request a Specific Roommate?"

Colleges may offer your child the option of specifying a roommate, and it may be tempting for him to do so. Going to school with one of his best friends from home can be an initial buffer against homesickness and loneliness, particularly if he is going far from home; living with a friend removes the uncertainty of dealing with a stranger. One parent never forgot the view from her own daughter's doorway—across the hall was a perfectly decorated room with matching bedspreads and a lifetime of pictures lining the walls.

In fact, when the situation presents itself, it may seem hard to resist. Before encouraging your child to room with someone he already knows, however, be sure he asks himself:

- How close a friend is it? How well do they know one another?
- Have they ever traveled or lived together before? For how many consecutive days? (School lasts more than a weekend!)
- Is the idea coming from both of them?
- Are they both open to meeting new people, or will one be jealous if the other makes new friends?

Be sure that both parties really want to share a room. When asked by a high school friend to room together at college, one student was reluctant to turn down a pal's request. But within a week of living together, it was patently obvious that the two roommates were completely incompatible. A 15-year friendship was severely strained, and perhaps permanently damaged.

An entirely different situation can arise when you know sons and daughters of *your* friends who will be going to the same school. Your child may not even have met them. You might well think that all of the positives of specifying a roommate still apply, but there can be major drawbacks as well. No matter how close your friendship, no matter how many good things you have heard about the child, he is still a stranger to your child. Unless you can arrange for your children to meet and spend time together beforehand, it is wise to use caution. The decision about whether to request a specific roommate should come from your child. Mutual requests are never challenged, and

every effort is made to pair those students. This magnifies the
need to explore compatibility ahead of time.

A STRANGER IS WAITING

"As soon as my daughter got the letter with her freshman
roommate's name, I wanted her to pick up the phone and call,
but she kept refusing. Finally, she burst into tears and cried,
'Suppose she doesn't like me.'"
"What a jerk!" Comment of a freshman after talking for the
first time with his roommate.

Sometime before you leave for campus, your child will receive the name and address of his roommate(s). Unless he has
decided to live with someone he already knows, encourage him
to make contact before he gets to school. Communicating with
a prospective roommate can serve as an icebreaker and help
ease the transition to a new environment.

If your child seems hesitant about picking up the phone,
don't take it as a sign of unfriendliness. Whatever his professed
excuse, he may actually be nervous about finding out what his
roommate is like—and vice versa. Just a name on a piece of
paper may trigger preconceived ideas in his mind. Instead of
hounding him to call, suggest factual, practical questions that
might make it easier for him to initiate a conversation:

- What nonpersonal items is the roommate bringing? Communicating beforehand can prevent unnecessary duplica-
  tion of phones, answering machines, stereos, etc.
- When will the roommate(s) be arriving on campus? It may
  be possible to avoid problems about dividing the room if
  everyone arrives about the same time (see Chapter 5).
- Who will be coming with him, or is he coming alone?

If the phone number is unlisted or if your child is still
reluctant to start a conversation, a letter (with a home telephone
number) can substitute.

It's natural to imagine what a roommate will be like based
on his name and home address—but don't jump to conclusions,
nor should you be worried if you can't find the hometown on

a map. One family spent hours poring over the atlas looking for an unfamiliar town only to discover it was just a post office box in an adjoining state.

Caution your student about first impressions. If the initial contact between the roommates is less than impressive, chalk it up to nervousness on *both* parts. Good roommate relationships can take time to build.

GETTING TO KNOW YOU

"The truth is that my child is a slob—and his roommate let him know it."

"I never would have tried out for a part in a college theatrical production, except that my roommate was so involved that I thought I'd give it a shot."

What is a good roommate? Does such an individual even exist? Yes, he does, and, if prepared, your child could be one. For all the roommate jitters expressed by entering freshmen (and their parents), there seems to be little discussion about how to *be* a good roommate. Your child's abilities, talents, tastes, and personality traits are in place, and what he does with them in relation to a stranger is the essence of being a roommate.

It's important to talk with your student about what it means to be a good roommate. Here are some points to emphasize:

- Have an early discussion about important issues (non-negotiables), but with an understanding that they must become to some degree negotiables.
- Tolerance is the key to a successful roommate relationship. The two of you don't have to like the same things or people, but you do have to respect each other's choices.
- Remember that, at least in the beginning, your roommate is a stranger. Don't vent your anger or frustrations on him.
- Don't expect too much from your roommate. It's wonderful if your roommate is also your best friend, but that's just a bonus. Sometimes the best roommate is someone with whom you can just comfortably share quarters, but who leads an entirely separate life.

- Respect each other's need for a certain level of neatness and privacy. Some students have never had to share a room with anyone before—give that person some "space."
- Don't borrow anything from your roommate without expressed approval.
- During exam time, expect everyone's nerves to be on edge. Good humor and an extra degree of tolerance are essential—especially when your schedules are different. Don't have a party in the room when you're finished and he still has one to go.
- Stand up for your rights—but pick your battles. If your roommate's behavior is seriously disruptive, make clear your objections.
- Generally avoid direct competition with your roommate.
- Roommates as rivals for the same date, grade in a class, role in a play, job, etc., is generally just asking for trouble.

Roommates Play Different Roles

When completing the college's roommate compatibility questionnaire, one shy freshman asked to room with someone more outgoing. He hoped his roommate would help balance his own insecurity. It's not a bad idea—but students need to be realistic about what a roommate can and can't do. Perhaps having a more social roommate will encourage your student to be more outgoing, but each person's basic personality is set. It's unrealistic, and unfair, to expect a roommate to include your child in all his plans, to worry about his social (or academic) life, or to act as Svengali and transform him into something he's not.

But roommates sometimes fall into different patterns. One may be the leader, while the other appears to be a follower— and the roles may reverse during the year and even from one situation to another. Assuming that your child is comfortable with whichever role he takes (and that he's not sacrificing his own needs to please someone else), parents should stay out of it.

What About the Roommate Who Doesn't Participate?

One student complained that his roommate spent more time on the phone with his girlfriend at another school than he did in class. Another freshman quickly discovered that her room-mate was seriously depressed and rarely left the dorm except for class and meals.

Whatever the reason, if your student's roommate chooses not to participate in college life, your child should not feel responsible or change his own plans. Furthermore, it's not his job to act as amateur psychologist if he suspects there is a serious problem. Suggest that your student discuss any questions about his roommate's emotional or physical health with a resident advisor. There is nothing that an RA has not heard before.

Parents of Roommates

You now have something very much in common with people who may have been complete strangers just a short while ago—children living together under a roof separate from yours. If one of you lives closer, there may come a time when you'll host the roommate in your home or provide medical referrals in an emergency. When your child goes to school more than a few hours' drive from home, there's a certain comfort zone in having someone you know closer to campus than you are, as well as a reciprocal pleasure in being able to give that help yourself.

You will certainly want to keep the other parents' phone number handy, and you may even find that you build a telephone friendship. In some cases, you might also receive calls asking about their child's activities or whereabouts. Generally, don't put yourself—or permit your student to be put—in the middle of the other family's dispute.

One mother got a late-night phone call from the parents of her child's roommate inquiring whether the two of them were on campus or on a road trip. The truth was that both had left campus several days earlier—but only one set of parents had been informed. The roommate had deliberately kept her own parents in the dark. The mother answered the question honestly, but felt that she had betrayed a confidence in revealing where the students were. In retrospect, she decided it would have been better had she spoken only about her own student's whereabouts.

WHOSE ROOM IS IT?

"Every time my son taped a message for the answering machine, his roommate erased it and replaced it with a recording of his own."

"For my daughter, the final straw was when she came back to her room late one night and found a drunken stranger snoring in her bed—it was her roommate's guest."

However nervous your child may be about living on his own with complete strangers, those jitters often pale beside your own. After all, until now you've usually known his friends and often their families. If he were getting married, you would at least have had some time to get used to his prospective mate and to satisfy yourself that all will be well—or at least learn to adjust. College is different. Not only won't you be there, but you may not even hear how things are going unless there is a real problem—and even then your child may not share the situation until it becomes a crisis. You've always hoped he would learn your values, and now you've got to worry about what effect living with a stranger is going to have on all those lessons. Ever since your child started the college application process, you've heard horror stories about roommates and dorm living—or at least you've been paying more attention to them. It's hard to understand (or accept) the idea that you can't do anything about the lifestyle or behavior of your child's roommate—after all, you paid for half the room, didn't you? True, but the roommate's parents paid for the other half, and you don't own the room.

A New England college administrator pointed out her frustration at receiving a telephone call from an irate parent before the student even arrived on campus. The school had failed to give his son the best dorm there. The father was a major contributor. Next came the telephone call from the college president stating that he, too, had heard from the perturbed parent. This type of behavior is not uncommon, but the administrator stood firm (standard procedure in all schools), and, despite his father's concern, the student was happy throughout freshman year.

Parental pressure can preconceive problems, but there is really no way to predict that success or failure, happiness or loneliness in college will result from roommate matching or dorm placement. In reality, schools don't have extra space to allow for moving around the children of unhappy parents. Although you can certainly show concern and raise questions, you are now considered a third party. Encourage your student to ask his own questions and to explore different options.

Clashing Value Systems

As parents, we've learned that you don't have to agree with your neighbor on much of anything, but you do need mutual respect. At the very least, we would hope that our children can coexist with their roommates.

Unfortunately, problems can arise by nature of the fact that lifestyle issues, which may have been moot for the high school student, come to the fore when he is living on his own. Suppose that it's the worst case scenario. Your student and his roommate are truly incompatible, and it's more than a question of just not liking one another. Social life and/or academic performance are being adversely affected; there may be serious health or lifestyle issues at stake. Can your child request reassignment? How long does he have to wait before making a switch?

Depending on the school and how tight its housing situation, the answer can range from yes to absolutely no. One college prided itself on a "20-minute rule." If a student was unhappy with his roommate, he could move within 20 minutes. Some schools will give your child a list of available space and allow him the option of finding another roommate. Other schools insist that nothing short of attempted murder would be sufficient reason to allow a switch in rooms.

Of course, the first step to resolving any problem is to encourage your child to talk it out with his roommate. This is often met with a flat "I can't." Confrontation doesn't come easily for some students. Still, as a parent, you need to point out the obvious: "No one is a mind reader," and the roommate may not realize that his behavior or habits are unpleasant or even obnoxious. Sometimes it's a clash of lifestyles, upbringing, temperament, or even cultures. Preaching tolerance is important, but it's equally vital that your child realize that he needs to stand up for his rights while remembering the rights of his roommate.

Mediation is the next step. Colleges are prepared to help with roommate problems, even if they're unprepared to move them. Your student's resident advisor or the housing office can require even an unwilling roommate to participate in mediation.

While it would be nice if roommates could work out the kinks in the relationship informally, it sometimes helps literally to spell things out. On many campuses the college staff is trained to negotiate clear contracts covering the details of everyday life in the room, including neatness, guests, study time, and music. A recent graduate remembered that her freshman roommate was so messy that a line was literally drawn down the center of the room—and it was never crossed.

Sometimes even a contract doesn't work, and students simply spend very little time in the room. As one freshman commented, "In a bad situation, a good roommate stays away from the room as much as possible." It's somewhat similar to the "cheap lodgings" approach to travel: "Who cares what the room is like? I'm so busy touring that I'm only going to sleep there." Students study in the library, use the computer center for doing papers, and meet friends elsewhere. This solution rarely satisfies parents, but students often adapt easily.

One freshman, unable to cope with his roommate's parade of overnight guests, spent his nights and most of his free time in a friend's room down the hall. While this resolution enraged his parents because they had paid for half the room, the student was quite content with the way he had handled the situation.

TIP: Don't encourage your child to switch rooms unofficially.

It's tempting to applaud when your unhappy child moves lock, stock, and barrel into another room, but schools frown on this. For one thing, it may be impossible to contact him in the event of an emergency, and, in fact, it may even constitute a violation of the student judicial code or a housing code at the college. Although the sanction differs from one campus to another, options include fines, a stipulation on future room assignments (meaning your child will be at the bottom of the list for preferred space), or even a forced move back to the original room. If your student finds a more compatible living situation, be sure he informs his resident advisor and works out the necessary changes with him, or notifies the housing office.

One mother didn't know exactly what to do when her daughter reported that she had entered her dorm room and discovered her roommate and another woman in an intimate embrace. After calling the dean of the college, the mother was surprised to learn that the college would not switch her daughter's room because there had never been any suggestion of impropriety by the roommate toward her daughter. Sexual orientation, said the college, was not a reason to switch rooms. It was vitally important that the young woman and her parents discuss the situation and how she should handle it, especially in light of the college's policies. They decided as a family that the girl would move off campus for the remainder of the semester.

RESIDENT ADVISORS: THE VOICE OF EXPERIENCE

"When my daughter woke up in the middle of the night with a 103 degree fever, the RA accompanied her to the health center."

"I called the RA when my son's grandfather died. He helped my child make arrangements to come home for the funeral and saw that he got the notes for any missed classes."

One person you'll probably meet on move-in day is your child's resident advisor (RA), also called dorm counselor, proctor, peer counselor, or a number of other titles. On most campuses this will be an enthusiastic upperclassman or graduate student, usually chosen by college administrators for his ability to reach out and help incoming students during the freshman adjustment period. He will often be the one who can offer the kind of support network a family would at home. If the RA doesn't have the answer to a question or problem, he will know who does.

The resident advisor will be the one your child can go to for anything from juggling schedules and campus activities to dealing with simple homesickness or quarters lost in laundry machines. When you meet him, ask whether his position requires that he stay on campus over the weekend. If your child runs into problems then, an RA can be a lifesaver.

REMEMBER: Get the resident advisor's campus phone number in case you have to contact your child in an emergency.

If your child is having problems with his roommate, encourage him to go to his resident advisor for advice. The RA has most likely seen (and handled) just about any kind of issue that might be in question. He'll also be able to bring a dispassionate view to the situation and perhaps assure that things don't get out of hand.

The RA will help communicate campus (and housing) rules, but will generally not act as a police officer to enforce regulations. In more serious situations, a resident advisor might turn to a freshman dean or dean of students to help (or discipline) your child. When a matter reaches this stage, you might be called or made aware of the student's inability to conform. Rules vary from campus to campus, and each college's approach to maintaining the code varies as well.

The main role parents will play in this process is, again, as supportive, friendly sounding boards. You can listen to your student, sympathize, even make suggestions, but in most cases, it is up to him to resolve the problem. It's tempting to rush to the phone and call the dean, but as with much of college life, the college wants to hear, at least at first, from the student, not the parent. Keep in mind, too, that you may be more upset about a roommate's behavior than your child is. As one freshman neatly described the situation, "These problems seem larger to parents; students cope."

As with much of college, you may not always agree with your child's choices, but if he is comfortable with the decision, your role as parent is to keep quiet.

SETTING UP SHOP|5

"After loading and reloading the car several times, we were finally all stuffed in and ready to go. Three tension-filled hours later we arrived and found out that the fridge we had managed to shove in the trunk could have been rented there for less money than we had paid and the box we had left in the front hall for shipping had her sheets and pillowcases. After lugging everything up the stairs, we stood there shuffling our feet and tried not to cry—we failed miserably. After a great deal of hugging, my daughter told us we could go, so we made the return trip home—only to hear the phone ring as we walked in the door. My daughter wanted to know where we were—she had only wanted us to go to the motel so she could take a nap before dinner."

You've lived through the applications, the agonizing wait for admission letters, the late-night conversations about which school your child will choose, the shopping, and the packing. Now it's time to take your child to college.

Sad, excited, worried, relieved, sanguine, depressed, your emotions run the gamut—and vary from individual to individual. Many parents feel overwhelmed, and almost everyone feels exhausted. In one family, the tensions throughout senior year in high school had been so intense, the parent-child battles so numerous, that while the adults knew they would miss their son, it was frankly a relief to know that they would soon have him out of the house.

Part of the sadness you may be feeling is the recognition that you are really saying goodbye twice. First, of course, it's literally saying farewell to your child as he embarks, solo, on a new adventure. Secondly, although it sounds melodramatic, you realize that you are ending a chapter in your family life. If there is any comfort in this situation, it is the knowledge that while your family life will never be quite the same, it can be as rich and fulfilling as those early years when your child lived at home. Change won't necessarily be stark and dramatic. But it may take time for you to believe that.

This chapter focuses on one 24-hour period: when you take your student to college, unpack everything you've been organizing for months, meet the roommate (and his family), attend orientation meetings for parents, and then say goodbye. It's a jam-packed time, fraught with emotion.

GETTING THERE

"We pulled up in front of the dorm in a big, red convertible, the only car available at the airport rental counter—my daughter was mortified."

"We opted to drive for seven straight hours—the alternative was a flight to a nearby large city, a two-hour wait for a smaller plane, and a cab to the campus."

Travel to school will, to some extent, be dictated by distance and campus accessibility. How far are you willing to drive and how much time can you afford to spend getting there? Some families arrange to take vacations along the route or in the area of the college. Others won't have that much flexibility. Parents may not be able to take much time off from work and from home responsibilities. If your child has a job that requires him to work until just before school, you'll have to figure out whether the distance is truly manageable by car in the time available. Whether you drive or fly, however, there are some basic points to keep in mind.

PLAN AHEAD

1. If you are renting a minivan or small truck, reserve it a month or more in advance.

2. Check on the availability of a one-way rental for small trucks, with a drop-off option near the college—have your child or another family member drive your car so it's available for the return trip.

3. Arrange for secured (locked and guarded) overnight parking for your vechicle and its contents if you will be staying anywhere overnight.

4. Make airline reservations early—check the price difference for adding a Saturday-night stay if you can manage the time. Confirm reservations within 48 hours of departure.

5. Don't forget to reserve in advance for a rental car at the airport if you will need one for transportation while you are there.

6. If you will be staying overnight, make motel/hotel reservations early.

Setting a Departure Date

Although some families plan vacation around the move to college, tread carefully around the issue of how soon you leave home, and discuss the pros and cons with your child. Don't assume that his reactions will be the same this summer as they have always been. Start by finding out whether he will be the first or the last of his friends to leave. If he is the first, it will not be easy to schedule a trip that takes him away from home even earlier than he expected.

One family thought their child would welcome the fact that they had managed to squeeze in enough days off to go on their annual trip to the shore on the way to school. It turned out that their daughter made a special detour back in order to see her best friend before actually setting out for college. If, on the other hand, your child is one of the last to leave, his hometown begins to seem empty to him, and he is likely to become more amenable—and even anxious—to hit the road.

Sometimes, parents have not seen the campus or the area around it and would like to use this opportunity to travel. If this is the case, and your child is reluctant to leave home early enough, tack the extra days onto your trip after you move him into his dorm.

Whether or not you arrange vacation to coincide with taking your child to college, there are advantages to arriving before the actual move-in time. You'll give yourself some breathing room to buy any last-minute items you may have forgottten, and you'll also avoid the long lines for taking care of business details:

- Setting up telephone service and any other electrical hookup
- Banking (if you haven't opened an account by mail)
- Opening bookstore and other charge accounts
- Shopping for/purchasing computers
- Buying books and supplies
- Registering for a student ID
- Picking up room keys

Although colleges have different schedules for doing all of this (and not all schools require each of these items), the lines get longer and the service may become more harried as the time gets closer to the opening day of school. Some students even find that they can do part of this business a day earlier than specified on the orientation schedule—check the campus as soon as you arrive, and you may be pleasantly surprised.

On the other hand, if you cannot get there before the dorms open, you are not necessarily at a disadvantage. Some of the above list may be taken care of by your student *after* you leave, when the lines are certain to be shorter. One new freshman saw the crowd in the computer store and decided to pick up her preordered machine the following week. There may be other details that can be taken care of later, and it's a good idea not to put too much pressure on an already hectic day.

You won't be able to avoid all lines, but if you do spend time waiting for service, remember that those around you are part of the same pool—first-year students and their parents. It's an opportunity to meet many of them, share information, and perhaps even form some friendships. One mother met a contemporary who had graduated from *her* college 25 years earlier—and she felt better immediately. If your child is somewhat nervous, he may well be put at ease when he meets other freshmen who feel the same way.

Whatever you decide about arriving on campus, remember to choose the way that is going to fit your family best—some avoid crowds, lines, hassles at any cost; others can't afford extra time away from home or business.

The Last Night at Home

You and your student may have very different plans for how he will spend the last evening at home.

TIP: No matter what he does, or with whom, it is wise for him to keep the partying to a minimum.

You both have a big day ahead, and most schools plan a full complement of activities for the opening week at college. You want your student rested and ready to plunge in with both feet—and exhaustion only adds to the tension.

While you may want to spend the last night at home as a family, he may want to spend it with friends. One possible compromise is to have dinner as a family, and then he can meet his friends later. As one mother explained her motives for fussing over dinner, "I wanted to make everything pleasant, and I cooked all his favorite foods. That way I figured he would *want* to come home again."

But be aware that tensions are running high and that emotions are near the surface for your student (and you), so don't be surprised at bickering and snapping. Younger siblings are also feeling confused and worried about all the changes and may respond by arguing with you or the departing freshman. It would be nice if everyone behaved like a TV family from the fifties, but we all know that rarely happens. One father was so grumpy the night before he took his daughter to school that she finally asked, "Are you acting that way so I'll be glad to leave home?"

FROM A CAST OF THOUSANDS TO
TRAVELING SOLO

"I never thought my ten-year-old would want to take a six-hour ride in the car—until I saw the look on her face when we were leaving without her."

"It was a question of going to the quarterly budget review or taking my child to college—and my job was paying for the tuition."

Deciding when to go and how to go may be the easiest decisions you'll have to make. Deciding who, if anyone, goes along can present unexpected problems.

Siblings Too?

Many younger siblings want to be part of the caravan that escorts your child off to school—but there may be limits on the number you include, if any. Certainly, age is a consideration, and the sibling may have already started school. Beyond that, do you literally have the room, and for how many? If you are driving, there may barely be room in the packed car for the student, let alone anyone else. When you are flying, the expense of extra tickets may influence your decision. Aside from transportation, there will be costs for lodging if you decide to spend more than one day at the college. If finances are a question, you may have to balance the cost of a baby-sitter against the cost of bringing the sibling(s).

You may also prefer to leave siblings at home, if possible, because of all the details and activities that will require your attention when you get to campus. It's hard to sit through a parent orientation program on practical college majors that lead to successful careers with a nine year old tugging at your sleeve. Furthermore, this can be an emotional time for both you and your first-year student, and you may simply want some time alone with him. Having younger siblings along may limit you and may even be boring for them.

Of course, there are advantages to bringing "the family." Don't underestimate the attachment of brothers or sisters to your freshman (see Chapter 7)—and don't think explanations of how bored they will be will smooth over hurt feelings. They (and your student) may have to sort through their own emotions just as you sort through yours. Bringing siblings has its practical side as well. One younger sister ignored the turmoil around her and calmly began to unpack boxes.

If you decide to bring siblings, tell them *before* you go what they will be doing when they get there, what kind of help you will be expecting from them, and what your expectations are for their behavior. Be sure they understand that, at least on this trip, they must take second place.

If you won't be including siblings in the trip, explain why they must stay home and arrange for them to have some one-on-one time with your college child before he leaves. It wouldn't hurt to emphasize the prospect of being shepherded from place to place with no time for much fun!

When Your Child Goes Alone

A lasting memory for one parent was the sight of his son's new roommate arriving alone in an airport cab with one suitcase; the rest of the boxes had been shipped—and were now in a depot across campus. Some children have to travel to campus by themselves for a variety of reasons, and it doesn't have to be a disastrous experience. If you're not going with your child:

- Find out from the housing office whether the college has any special arrangements for students arriving alone.
- Where possible, arrange for family or friends to meet him and perhaps house him the night before move-in if he is coming a long way.
- Plan the simplest, most direct route, even if it is more expensive (unless he is used to traveling).
- If he is going by plane, check for airports that might be smaller but closer to the school; have a contingency plan in case he is delayed along the way and misses a flight or connection.
- Give him a phone number where he can reach you if you won't be home.
- Be clear about when you want him to call you—and realize that his phone may not be hooked up and that he may have to use an outside public phone.

- Make sure that some or all of his boxes arrive on campus before he does. In case they don't, be sure he has a bag with him that includes a set of sheets, a towel, and a change of clothes.

It's a good idea for him to let his roommate know in advance that you won't be there—and to find out whether the other parents will be. But don't expect them to assume responsibility for your child, because they may have their own plans. Before your student leaves home, talk to him about setting up his section of the room and encourage him to stand up for his rights if his roommate (or his roommate's parents) seem overbearing.

If you are bringing your child to school and his roommate is alone, make an effort to stand back and let them be one on one, instead of lending your weight and authority to your own child. While you want to be helpful and supportive of the child who is alone, avoid the temptation to become an instant parent. You don't really know the roommate and have no idea how independent he is or how sensitive about accepting help. If possible, decide ahead of time whether you will be including him in your plans for dinner, etc., so that you can avoid awkward situations.

What If Only One Parent Can Go?

It may not be possible for both parents to take the child to campus. If this means that you think you will need help when you get there, be sure to find out whether the college provides this or whether you will have to plan for assistance on your own.

The normal strain of leaving for college may be compounded for families where there has been a divorce or separation. Rather than force the situation, consider having one parent take the child to campus and the other spend a weekend shortly after school begins.

In any case, encourage your child to call the one who didn't accompany him within the first few days so that he can share move-in experiences.

ARRIVAL

"We pulled up in front of the dorm, and it reminded me of curbside check-in at the airport. My husband drove away to find a parking space, and I stood there with my daughter, huddled under an umbrella in the pouring rain."

"It was a beautiful, new, ten-story dorm—with one broken elevator."

Imagine a neighborhood with anywhere from a hundred to thousands of new families moving in during one brief time span. People, cars, trucks, boxes—a logistical puzzle for those who are arriving and certainly for those who are making room for them. College move-in day is very much the same kind of experience, and although the length of time can vary from a couple of hours to an entire day, you will not soon forget it.

First Impressions Can Be Misleading

Even if you visited the campus with your child when he was considering applying to the school—or during the pre-frosh days after he was accepted—you see things through a different prism when you bring him to begin his college career. The bulletin boards will probably be full of announcements of campus groups eager to recruit new members. If the weather is nice, the quads are full of students chatting, throwing a frisbee, possibly holding an impromptu yard sale for the incoming freshmen.

One mother worried about what *she* should wear on move-in day. She wanted to make a good impression on the roommate, his family, and the dean during freshman convocation. Above all, make sure that you are comfortable. At the end of moving a ton of clothes, books, computer and stereo equipment, etc., into your student's room, you'll be hot, sweaty, and dirty. If there are orientation programs for parents, you may want to bring a change of clothing to freshen up.

You may be surprised at the number of groups visible on campus and worry whether your child will find an activity that's right for him. Some of the more politically active clubs may have the most, or most outrageous, posters—but there is undoubtedly a niche that is right for your student.

Similarly, the students on the campus may look cleaner—or grungier—than your child. One student was worried because it seemed that all the girls she saw on campus wore flats, while she preferred sneakers. The first people you see may not be representative of the group your student will seek out for his friends, but he will eventually find his way to the right mix for him.

Heave-Ho

As soon as you know where your child will be living, you can decide how much you can reasonably carry to the room in that one visit.

TIP: Buy, rent, or borrow a "dolly" to transport boxes from car to room.

If he is on a high floor, or if the weight of the boxes is a concern, find out whether there is an elevator and whether any help will be available on campus that day. At some schools, upperclassmen assist freshmen so that parents do not have to bear the heaviest loads. Where help is not officially provided, you might still be able to find a willing student for hire. If there is no help, consider having the heavier boxes delivered at a later time.

Pay attention to the kind of weather you can expect on move-in day. If it's going to be very hot and humid, or if it's likely to be pouring rain, you might also want to unload and carry only the necessary minimum.

TIP: Don't leave boxes unattended while parking the car.

Of course, this entire process is a learning experience. After lugging box after box up three flights of stairs, one parent noticed that those arriving at upperclass dorms didn't seem to be nearly so overburdened—not only had they stored some of their things, but they had learned just how little they really needed in the beginning. After all, no one can wear a year's worth of clothes in the first two weeks, and much of what is packed can actually be sent later.

Some campuses have extended periods of time for moving into freshman dorms. You'll be able to make your travel arrangements without worrying about long lines outside the dorm (the entire process will be much more spread out), and if the lines *are* long, you can choose to come back later. Before making your plans, check the orientation schedule so you won't miss a program you're interested in if it is going on during the move-in period.

If your child has this option, be sure he finds out when his roommate will be arriving so that they can make joint decisions about the room. Some colleges even stipulate in their orientation information that all occupants of the room be present before it is "divided." Unfortunately, not everyone pays attention to this wise note, and there are those who claim beds or totally arrange one side of the room before the other person is there—certainly not the best way to begin a relationship. A more creative solution was that of a student who was moving into a suite with four other freshmen. Instead of waiting for the fifth person to arrive, he suggested that they save time by drawing room positions from a hat.

When the college has brief, specific hours for moving into the dorms, your flexibility is more limited, but you won't have the problem of waiting for a roommate to get there before making decisions. It's a fast, efficient process, but lines will be long, staircases will be packed—and parking will be limited. In this scenario, however early you arrive doesn't seem early enough to be at the head of the line. Despite the crowds, though, rest assured that everyone really does get moved in and somehow it all works out!

TIP: If you get there much earlier in the day (or even the day before), check out the parking facilities and the location of the dorm.

OVER THE THRESHOLD

"I couldn't help but feel deflated when I saw my son's room."
"I felt so inadequate—the other father had already assembled a bookcase and was hanging the drapes when I arrived."

Armed with stories from other parents about freshman dorms, you're going to feel delighted, relieved, or disappointed the first time you see your child's new "home." If it is less than you had hoped, don't openly judge its size or location: There is nothing you can do about it, and extended negative comments may only make your student feel worse if he is already turned off about what he sees. Then again, he may be viewing the room through the rose-colored glasses of independence and not see any of the drawbacks that you do.

REMEMBER: It's his room in his dorm, not his room in your house.

It may be tempting to tell your child which side of the room to take and how to position his desk. You may also feel embarrassed about his choice of decorations, and consider his posters to be outrageous or even distasteful. Worse yet, you may be uneasy about his *roommate's* taste. One mother was concerned when she walked into her son's room on move-in day and discovered that his roommate had "decorated" with beer paraphernalia, heavy-metal posters, and a biker helmet labeled "death" perched on the windowsill. Her son, however, tacked up his football pennants on the other side of the room—and a beautiful friendship began! Hard as it may be, this is the time to step back unless your child asks for your advice. Whatever decisions he has to make about his living space will be that much more difficult if you are adding your opinion.

You'll certainly want to help unpack, discard unnecessary cartons, stow away duffel bags, make the bed, check the outlets, hook up electrical equipment (stereo, computer), plug in lamps—there's more than enough work for everyone! Let your child take the lead as much as possible, though. Don't assume that he will simply recreate his room at home.

Renovation and Interior Design

Anticipating old but comfortable rooms behind the ivy-covered walls of the dorm, one family was shocked when they entered and found other parents wielding paintbrushes on dingy walls. As one mother asked, "For $25,000, they expect me to paint?" They viewed their own son's room as serviceable, but questioned the positioning of the beds shoved together against one wall. How much should you expect to do, and how much can you do?

Dorm conditions will vary from college to college and even within a campus; newer isn't necessarily better, older doesn't guarantee character, and cleanliness really is the standard you are seeking. Realistically, the state of the dorm seems to bother parents more than students.

MOVE-IN DAY SUPPLIES

Pack supplies to clean the dorm room before your student puts away his belongings. You will want to wipe down the mattress, bookshelves, and the insides of the closet and drawers. You'll need:

1. Disinfectant

2. Sponge/paper towels/dust cloth

3. WD-40 to unstick desk or bureau drawers

4. Hammer and screwdriver to open painted-shut windows, put unassembled equipment together, and affix items to the wall, if allowed

5. Bottled water, juice, and snacks—since move-in day is hectic and usually hot

---

Beyond housekeeping, don't make plans for elaborate remodeling without reviewing the school's regulations (spelled out in a housing contract), which will stipulate what can and cannot be done to the room.

TIP: If the contract allows for "remodeling," so long as the room is restored to its original state, be sure both roommates agree ahead of time on how any expense is to be divided and on what exactly they are going to do.

There is no one way to set up the room, and what you see may simply represent an arrangement that was easiest for the college cleaning staff. Look to maximize space:

- Bookcases can go atop desks, leaving just enough space for the computer (the printer goes below the desk).
- Cinder blocks (watch the weight!) raise beds from the floor to increase the storage space.
- Stackable cubes, used to transport things from home, can become handy storage units in the room.
- Trunks double as coffee tables.
- Closets hold more than clothes: Some are big enough for bureaus.

You may have a more practiced eye than your child, but don't jump right in with advice. Give him a chance to figure out solutions with his roommate—if they don't see all the possibilities, suggest a few and leave the final decisions to them. What seems like chaos on move-in day eventually sorts itself out, sometimes only after you've gone. It would not even be unusual for your child to rearrange his room several times during the year to accommodate changing study and social routines—or to leave it as is because he's perfectly comfortable even if you're not.

After You Unpack

Soft-sided duffel bags or even giant "body bags" can be folded and stored in the closet. There won't be room for many boxes (if any), though, and you'll have to get rid of them—the dorm may not have a place to keep them. (You may want to keep "specialized" boxes, like those in which the computer or stereo equipment was packed, for the return trip home at the end of the year. If there is no room for the empty boxes at the dorm, you may want to ask about other campus storage or take them home.)

Besides taking boxes away, be prepared to bring home some of what your child has brought. If roommates haven't been in touch, there may be too many phones, an extra answering machine, even a stereo. It's not wise to leave costly equipment in a dorm closet lest it be stolen.

What If It's All Done?

Despite your best intentions to stay neutral and allow your child to set up his own room, other parents may not be so amenable. One family arrived to find that the roommate had already claimed two-thirds of the space—and the father was busily constructing a sleeping loft for their son. Ideally, you'd like to encourage your child to deal with these situations himself. He and his roommate will be living there, and at this first meeting you don't know whether the other parents are acting for, or in spite of, their child. Provided that no housing rules are being broken by what is being done, don't take an active role. Keep in mind, too, that you may be more upset by what is happening than your child is.

Even if he seems uncomfortable with what's going on, however, he may not want to challenge the assertiveness of the other
parents. Encourage him to speak to his roommate, perhaps after
they are alone. Whatever remarks you decide to make, direct
them to the other parent and not the roommate. Don't start your
student's college career by running interference for him with
those his own age. Of course, you may have to step in if you see
that the other parent is violating the housing contract rules with
his alterations.

A Break from the Move

Along with a room key and directions to the dorm, you, as
the parent of an incoming freshman, will be handed a schedule
of events being offered on move-in day/weekend. These can
range from small informal hall mixers with an RA to audito-
rium-filled welcome speeches by the college president and
deans. If time allows and you are willing to crisscross the
campus, this could be your opportunity to establish a sense of
place—the place where your child will be living, learning, and
growing for the next four years. Colleges schedule many events
to give you a feel for the place, but they also realize the emotional push-and-pull going on these first few hours. Orientation
activities can actually help to distract you from the separation
anxiety you and your student may be feeling.

Colleges plan these programs carefully. This is not like back-
to-school night or the parent-teacher conferences of the past. It
is designed to show you—and reassure you—about educa-
tional and residential college life. After attending a panel discussion led by faculty "stars," one father remarked how calm
and "laid back" the professors seemed to be on an otherwise
hectic move-in day. On the other hand, he attributed their
relaxed attitude to the fact that these professors had not been
up since the crack of dawn, had not driven for hours, and had
not unloaded an 18-year-old's lifetime's worth of belongings
into a cramped cubicle!

In addition to academic programs, first-day choices (for parents and/or students) can include athletic events, tours of the
campus and/or the college health center, panel discussions on
campus security, music or theatrical performances, scientific

programs, collegiate organization forums, meals, snacks, picnics, and access to a host of upperclass volunteers and college administrators. If orientation occurs over a weekend, there will probably be services and programs offered by the various religious denominations (see Appendix I).

Whether you choose to attend one, many, or none of the planned activities is up to you. Some parents, giving their students some breathing room, choose to go alone to an event. Others will have their student accompany them on the round of activities. Remember that your child may be focused on setting up his room, scheduled for some dorm meeting, or intent upon connecting with other freshmen.

IS YOUR STUDENT SAFE ON CAMPUS?

"My son's roommate was mugged the first week of school when he made an ATM withdrawal late at night at an off-campus location."

"My daughter reported to campus security that her pearl necklace was missing, only to find it in her room, under a tremendous pile of dirty clothes."

They're not home anymore. You can't check their beds to see if they are tucked in, safe and sound. One mother confessed that she still woke up at night in a panic wondering where her son was and what he was doing—even after he had been in school for six months.

Parental worries about security on campus are a common and reasonable concern. While he was living at home, you may have been the one responsible for locking the doors or turning on a home alarm system. Now your student must take responsibility for both his own personal safety and the security of his belongings.

Be sure to ask about the past record of campus security when you visit the school. Ask what measures the campus police have taken to ensure student safety. A 1992 Federal law requires colleges to disclose crime statistics each September, but numbers can be misleading. For example, thefts that do not involve breaking and entering are classified as larcenies and need not be reported. Thus, a stereo stolen from an unlocked dorm room would not be included in the school's security summary.

Furthermore, some schools choose to refer some crimes to college judiciary committees rather than the local police. This policy permits a student offender to avoid a criminal record but skews the campus security statistics, making the college appear safer than it really is. Finally, many experts believe that some crimes, such as sexual abuse and assault, are vastly underreported. While it's important that your student attend any security workshop during orientation, *and pay attention*, it's also vital that your child understand that he must be responsible for his own personal security.

Personal Safety

Even if the college campus is in a remote setting, your child should not ignore basic security measures. There used to be a tendency to see college campuses as safe and invulnerable against outside forces—but not anymore.

In order to minimize the risk of assault or rape, review personal safety guidelines with your child—even if he is a football linebacker or she rolls her eyes in silent protest that she "already knows all this stuff." Note that personal safety extends beyond the campus to wherever he might go to shop, eat, visit an ATM, or travel to another school. Tell your child to:

- Be realistic about the area surrounding the campus— know where it is safe to walk and at what hours.
- Note the location of emergency telephone boxes.
- Never walk alone at night, either on campus or off campus (this goes for males as well as for females). Use campus escort services at night if there is no one else around.
- Lock the dorm room when alone on the hall, and never admit a stranger, even if he purports to be another student.
- Check to see whether smoke alarms are functional—double-check the battery as the year progresses. Take note of emergency exits and procedures *before* there is a problem.
- Avoid being alone in isolated areas of the library, labs, or dorm laundry rooms. Don't exercise in the gym or jog on a track alone during the early morning or late evening hours. The "buddy system" is still the safest way.

- Don't be embarrassed to notify the campus security service of any suspicious people or events.

Keeping Property Secure

Beyond questions about personal safety, your student has to take precautions with his belongings.

NOTE: Assuming a worst-case scenario, check your homeowner's insurance policy to know your coverage for theft away from home.

Campus life may be more casual and open, but there are still basic security rules for protecting personal property. Your child should:

- Always lock the door to the dorm room, and don't lend the key to anyone.
- Never leave laundry unattended. Either stay in the laundry room throughout the wash and dry cycles (with a buddy) or check back frequently.
- Use a *locked* locker for belongings when using the campus gym.
- Always use a bicycle lock.

IT'S TIME TO SAY GOODBYE

"After we dropped our daughter at school, my husband cried the entire length of the turnpike. Finally, I pulled off the road, turned, and said, 'She didn't die; she went to college.'"

"I worried that something was wrong with our relationship. I wasn't at all tearful—and neither was my son."

How you react after you take your child to college is not necessarily indicative of your relationship. Some parents find it hard to keep their emotions in check, while others are more reserved or very excited about this new "adventure." You may feel any of these emotions, or any combination of them.

Sometimes a husband or wife is surprised by what appears to be a lack of emotion by the partner at this crossroads. Each member of the family deals with the separation in his own way and at his own pace. One father, cool as a cucumber during the previous weeks as well as on move-in day, spent the following night sleepless and depressed at all the opportunities and experiences he had missed in his child's life. He found no comfort in his wife's reassurances that he had been an excellent father.

When Is the Best Time to Leave?

Many schools answer the question for you. They build a suggested time for parents to depart into their orientation program. Usually it's after a major event, such as a picnic or freshman convocation, and before the start of some other program that will engage your child.

If it's up to you to time your leave, use the same strategy if possible. The idea is that your child will say his farewells and move on to something fun. If you must stay longer in the area for reasons of distance or expense, respect his privacy. One family, in order to get the most economical airfare, decided to remain in the metropolitan area of their son's college for two additional days. While he was perfectly willing to come to the hotel to say a final goodbye before they flew home, he was adamant that he didn't want the family to be seen on campus after all the other parents had left! Ironically, the family had intended to spend at least part of the extra time sightseeing but were so exhausted by the move-in experience that they saw very little.

There is an advantage to staying an extra day or two after the official farewells. One family felt it took the edge off the return trip home. Move-in day had been so exhausting, physically and emotionally, that they needed some time to recuperate before the long drive home. Their leave-taking didn't seem quite so dramatic as if they had left instantly. It was clear that they no longer had a role on campus, and they were only too glad to head back to *their* world.

Suppose I Cry?

The moment has arrived. It's time to leave. The best case scenario is a warm, quick hug, a few words of love, and then a goodbye. This is not the moment for any long reflections on what it all means. It's better if you can stave off the tears until you are alone. Your child may be fighting to keep himself together and may not be able to sustain it if he sees you cry.

On the other hand, if you fall apart—and it has happened to many people—that's okay, too. You'll all survive, and while you may be momentarily embarrassed, this too shall pass. It's one of those stories that your child will understand better when he has kids of his own. One mother ruefully recounts the conversation she had with her older daughter, who had received a plaintive telephone call from a freshman sibling: "Tell Mom to stop crying every time she sees me."

Suppose He Cries

"She had the same look on her face that she had when I left her at nursery school for the first time. Then she cried, and I sobbed." While the college schedule may suggest a time to leave, you know your child better than anyone else. If he is really having a hard time separating, you may want to extend your stay. Perhaps your child could attend a few of the orientation events and then meet you again later on, or if you must leave for home, set a time to talk by telephone that evening.

Homesickness and worry over fitting in are common freshman complaints. They are not a sign of immaturity. Some kids find move-in day exciting and fun, while others are overwhelmed by the whole process. Advise your child that if he feels homesick during his first night in the dorm, it's a normal reaction as he adjusts to new surroundings.

After months of anticipation, this is finally it. Your "baby" is at college. But getting him there was only half the battle. You probably feel many emotions at this moment, but chief among them will undoubtedly be exhaustion. One mother said it took her about a month after she took her son to college to realize how stressful the senior year of high school and the summer before college is for *parents*. From the pressures of applying to college, to the interminable wait for acceptance, through the shopping, packing, driving, unloading, and final emotional goodbyes, it had been a long haul.

But the work is not over yet. The first year of college will be a time of adjustment for everyone. The coming months will be a learning experience for freshman and family alike.

STAYING CONNECTED: | 6
THE TIES THAT BIND |

"I considered myself one of the lucky ones. My son called regularly, not with earth-shattering news, but just to talk about everyday things. Sometimes he seemed quiet, and I wasn't sure why, until one day I played back part of our conversation that had been accidentally taped on the answering machine. I listened to myself sounding very much like some kind of shrew. He was talking about all the work he was doing and had to do, and I asked—in an accusing tone—about the paper he hadn't started. He went on about winning a game, despite feeling weak with hunger during overtime, and I lectured about his eating habits. After listening to that tape, I decided I wouldn't want to call me!"

Once a student is away at school, parents need to establish new lines of communication. Phone calls and letters replace face-to-face conversations, where you can read the body language as well as hear the words. The challenge for parents is keeping in close enough contact with your child to understand

and appreciate the new experiences and pressures of student life, while respecting his growing need for privacy and independence. Not an easy task. More than ever, you need to pick up the subtle nuances in his voice and words to "hear" what he is *really* telling you.

Seemingly ever-present roommates complicate any phone call home. Your child may be reluctant to discuss anything too personal or revealing in front of peers. He may hesitate to disclose any problems or doubts because he is concerned with maintaining an image of competence and self-confidence, for you, for friends, and for himself. Your child may also be worried about sharing too much about his life because he is anxious about your reaction.

Conversely, you may be on the receiving end of daily phone calls, especially in the beginning of the year, expressing homesickness or confusion. He may not even actually verbalize any negative emotions but still feel the need to touch base frequently. How you handle these crises of confidence from a distance is a difficult balancing act.

COPING WITH HOMESICKNESS

"Because our son came home almost every weekend, we thought he missed us—until we realized that he spent most of his time with a high school girlfriend."

"My daughter starred in all her high school theater productions, but she couldn't even get a walk-on role in college. Freshman year was a series of tearful phone calls."

You can't tell which student will be hit with a bad case of homesickness. Even the child who has gone away to summer camp for years may suffer from bouts of the blues. Reassure your child that these feelings are pefectly normal. When he worries that "I feel like such a baby," or "I feel so dumb," insist that homesickness is *not* a symptom of immaturity.

Nor does homesickness necessarily start with the first day of school. Some students, caught up in the excitement of the opening weeks of college, seem to be adjusting well and are surprised when they begin to feel blue and miss home later in the semester. One freshman was confused when he felt incredibly homesick *after* Parents' Weekend. While he hadn't called home much at all in the first two months of school (much to his parents' regret), he now found a reason to call home every day for a week after his family's visit.

Who—and What—Do They Miss?

College students may be homesick for many things including, but not necessarily, parents. Your child may well miss you, even if, in your mind, he has spent the last few years ignoring you! He may be homesick for his siblings, even if he used to fight with them. Many college students long for the pets they left at home.

Sometimes, it's the environment or climate back home that they miss. They may be reacting to the switch from an urban to a rural milieu (or vice versa), or the weather may be depressing. One student from Texas found herself very despondent after enduring the "arctic" cold of the Northeast. She liked the school but hated the snow.

Friends, both those left in town and those who have gone off to other schools, are sorely missed. Friendships forged in high school, developed through the trials and tribulations of early adolescence, can be deep and valued. Now your college student must once again build the easy camaraderie he enjoyed with his high school buddies. It takes time to make new friends, and your student may feel lost without his old circle of friends to support him.

High school romances are another cause of homesick freshmen. If your student elects not to date others while away at school, he may find himself out of the social loop at college (see Chapter 8). Even if he does enter the dating scene, he may still miss the familiarity of an established relationship.

Last, he may miss not only people, but his old life. Student government presidents can't all win the elections in college. The prom queen may be outshined by what seems to her to be the reigning Miss America. One college freshman had to come to terms with such a reality as a first-year student. Although he had been the star quarterback on his high school team, he was not good enough to play college-level football. He had to adjust to the fact that "I used to be leading the team, but now I'm sitting in the stands." He missed the roar of the crowd and the thrill of the play.

Your student may just miss the comfort and familiarity of high school. It was a time when he knew what was expected of him. Now he must confront a whole new set of rules, situations, and people. It can be scary.

Possible Solutions

Time, of course, is the ultimate cure. As your student becomes more involved in school activities, as he makes new friends, he will become more comfortable and less concerned with what he has left behind. But of course, in the middle of a crisis, no one wants to hear that "this too will pass." Refrain from voicing this sentiment, even though you know it's true. Although it may be tempting to make an emergency trip to campus, as a general rule, *don't*. By "rushing to the rescue," parents may actually undermine a child's self-confidence in being able to cope.

In the meantime, the phone calls home can break your heart. Much of your job is simply to serve as a sounding board. Although it's tempting to offer suggestions for instant cures, much of what your child needs is just to hear a familiar voice. He gets comfort from his hometown cheering squad. One parent was surprised when her son called every day for the first month of school. He absolutely loved the place, was making new friends, had plunged into the hustle and bustle of college life—and yet, needed to touch base, if only for a few moments, each day.

These phone calls are not prolonging the homesickness, but rather allowing your child to smooth the transition to his new life. If your budget permits, continue the telephone contact until your child is ready to cut back on his own. Generally, even the most severe cases of homesickness are "cured" by Thanksgiving.

Sometimes a family friend who lives near campus can provide some much needed TLC. One freshman, 3,000 miles from home and feeling blue, felt much better after dinner out, away from campus, with old family friends. Be sure to keep in touch with parents you may meet who live near campus. They can also be an invaluable resource for cheering up your lonely student.

Should He Come Home?

Assuming the college is located within a reasonable distance from home, your student may want to come home on weekends. The problem with this solution is that if your youngster is home, he can't be making new friends and plunging into the myriad of activities available at school. On the other hand, he may well need the familiarity of home in order to succeed in the present. One family's compromise seems a good solution. They suggested that their daughter come home every other weekend. While the student faithfully followed that schedule for her entire freshman year, as her mother laughingly points out, "we haven't seen her since." By the end of her first year in school, the student had created a "life" for herself at college, with friends and activities that drew her in.

REMEMBER: Kids adjust to new situations in their own way and at their own pace.

Much like walking, talking, even toilet training, some kids do it quickly, while others are late bloomers. Adjusting to school may be a snap for some kids; for others it may take months. Look for signs of progress, rather than instant cures.

Suppose It Doesn't Go Away?

For many students, Thanksgiving is the time they make the transition to their new life. Home and reunited with high school friends, the student discovers that college life is more interesting, exciting, and definitely "freer" than life in their hometown. College life, where you can always find something to do—and someone to do it with—at any hour of the day, is more fun than parents who go to sleep at ten. Homesickness, when they return to college after the break, is less of a problem.

Occasionally, the adjustment to college is harder and lasts longer. If you don't see any progress over time, ask yourself:

- Is his homesickness impacting his school work?
- How is his health?

- Is he literally withdrawing from college life, limiting his social interaction?
- Are his complaints about himself or about the college, i.e., "I can't make friends" or "I hate living in this location"?
- Are there other circumstances that are influencing his response to school (parental divorce, illness, family move)?
- Was this his first-choice school, or is he still disappointed over his rejection from his preferred college?
- What is his roommate like? the dorm? the resident advisor?

REMEMBER: Trust your instincts. You know your child best of all.

If you really believe that your child is in trouble emotionally, that the adjustment to school is taking too long and is seriously impacting his life, *insist* that your child seek help.

Begin with a resident advisor, the freshman dean, a member of the college clergy, or even his high school counselor who already has a relationship with him. *Despite what your student believes, this is not the first time they've dealt with this situation—nor is his the worst case they've ever seen.* It's hard for many students to open up to a relative stranger, and they are often embarrassed that they are not coping as well as they believe everyone else is. But sometimes just hearing from someone other than your parents that many freshmen suffer from severe bouts of homesickness is reassuring.

The college health center is another good resource. Most have support groups of other students undergoing a similarly difficult time or can provide (either on-campus or off-campus) professional counselors. If your student cannot receive adequate help at school, however, arrange for him to see (or talk by phone) with a doctor at home.

KEEP IN MIND: It's no reflection on your parent-child relationship if your child does not seem homesick!

TELEPHONE PLANS

"We arrived home one Saturday night to find a message on the answering machine: 'Does anyone still live here?' my daughter asked in a plaintive voice."

"My son's roommate told his parents that communication is
a two-way street and that they shouldn't expect him to be the
one to do all the calling."

The cartoon in which someone is trying to stir a pot, shoo the
dog, set the table, and pay the paperboy—when the phone
rings—seems all too true when it comes to hearing from your
college child. Their schedules don't seem to match yours; what
is free time for them may not be free for you. Usually you are
so happy to talk to them at all that you overlook whatever
inconvenience it causes.

Some families have to deal with a stampede to the phone
when it rings, as siblings race to be first with their own news
and you feel that you will never get a word in. Then, again, how
are you going to speak privately with everyone on your end
trying to talk at once, and how private is private in a dormitory?

One parent found it more satisfying to call (or be called) in
the afternoon when no one else was around on either end.
Know your student's class schedule (see Appendix D), and try
to find a mutually convenient time for longer discussions—
without discouraging the spontaneous call when either of you
just feels like it.

Be sure your child remembers to take with him your home
and business numbers. Give him an alternate number in case
of emergencies. Similarly, ask that he phone you with another
number for contacting him whenever his phone is out of order.
If both parents will be away, he should have a copy of the
itinerary.

For students on a tight budget, calls home might be an
expense at the bottom of their list, and they may simply wait
for you to use "your" money for the long-distance telephone.
You may wonder if there isn't a simpler (and less expensive)
way to stay in touch. Somehow letters get written to classmates,
but when it comes to Mom and Dad, even preaddressed envelopes don't provide much incentive.

What to Talk About

Your family life is continuing, and it's important for your
child to feel connected to the homefront. Not only do you want
to know what is going on in *his* life, but you want to convey to

the freshman at school what is happening to his siblings, neighbors, friends, and so on. By keeping up with the news from home, your child isn't a stranger in his own home when he returns for vacation. On the other hand, remember that his patience for the minutiae of your everyday life is about as strong as it was when he lived at home.

Let him lead the conversation when talking about college life. While you may be bursting with questions, avoid the appearance of a "cross-examination." Pick up the clues from his voice when you've touched on an unwelcome topic. Obviously you want to share in this new life, but most adolescents value their privacy and want to decide what information they will share— and when. Limit the judgmental tone in your voice when you hear new adventures—or you may not hear many more.

Should you tell your child you miss him? Of course! Everyone likes to be wanted. But be careful that you don't overstress in your conversations the loneliness you may very well be feeling. It's a burden for your child—and one he can't do much about.

What If He Isn't In?

If your child isn't in his room when you call, be circumspect about any message you leave on an answering machine. Remember that the machine may serve several roommates, and therefore the message may not be private (roommates will have to listen to *all* the messages to get their individual notices).

Keep in mind too that any message can be replayed, so think about the words and tone you use. They can come back to haunt both you and your child.

TIP: Don't be hurt if your child doesn't return a call—he may not have gotten the message!

Should You Call?

One freshman neatly summarized the problem with parents calling students: "It may not be convenient, I'm probably not there, and I'm frequently not in the mood." Work out with your child, beforehand, whether you should call "just to chat." Obviously, if you need to get in touch with him, then you will.

TELEPHONE ETIQUETTE

If phone conversations are your primary method of communication, make the most of the calls.

1. Begin your discussions with good, noncontroversial news. Bringing up bad news immediately, unless it's absolutely necessary, puts a damper on the conversation.

2. Keep a list near the phone of the things you want to cover when your child calls. It's easy to forget, especially if it's a spontaneous conversation.

3. Don't ask a question if you don't want to hear the answer. While you want to share what is happening in your student's life, making constant value judgments will limit how open your child will be with you.

4. Don't monopolize the conversation with details about people your child doesn't know or like. But *do* talk about your life at home and share news about family and friends.

5. Save, as much as possible, any criticism about his lifestyle or grades until you can see him in person. A telephone call is the least productive way to have this type of conversation. You can't know who will walk into the room on his end putting constraints on the discussion.

6. Let your student determine how long you will talk. He may be pressed for time, have to study, or have other plans. On the other hand, if you consistently find your conversations with your freshman short and unproductive, schedule a new time for an uninterrupted chat.

Scheduled Calls, Spontaneous, or Both?

Some families establish a weekly time for the student and parents to talk by phone. The advantages are no missed calls, the ability to take advantage of the lowest rates, and a certain guaranteed level of communication. But be realistic about the time you set for the phone call. One freshman protested long and loud when her mother suggested a weekly call at nine o'clock in the morning. "Are you kidding? I don't get up until at least noon on Sundays."

Other families prefer to allow "nature to take its course." The student calls when he has something to say. You know your family and finances and can decide which works best for your situation. You can always change the system if you feel that you aren't hearing from your child enough.

If budget permits, many parents set a general schedule for calls (for example, "call sometime between 11 and 2 on Sundays"), while also encouraging the youngster to pick up the phone if something is troubling or exciting him.

Paying the Bill

With a range of long-distance carriers from which to choose, it's easy to become confused about the different discount plans available. The carrier used by the college may automatically discount calls made by students. If the discount is not automatic, find out how to apply for one.

When your student signs up for his phone service, consider the available options. If the monthly bill will include all calls made from his room or suite, suggest that the roommates work out a payment plan *before* the first call is made. On some campuses payment can be deducted automatically from an individual college or bursar account. It's not a good idea to do this unless the roommates know one another very well. The bill should be reviewed before it is paid.

NOTE: If the bill isn't paid, the school will cut off service.

When one freshman didn't call home for some time, her parents tried to reach her—only to find that her phone had been disconnected. She had ignored the warning about late payment and didn't regain service until she finally paid the bill in full.

Some students may have the option of having a general phone service charge—excluding long-distance calls—billed monthly to the room. In that case, your student would need some kind of prepaid phone card or else a calling card. There will be no hassles about whose call was whose and no need for reimbursement among roommates. But there is an additional charge each time a calling card is used after an initial set of "free" calls. Even if your child's school doesn't work phone service this way, you will be receiving many unsolicited offers for calling cards simply because you are the parent of a college-age student. The offers all tout being able to restrict use of the card to specified numbers, and if your child will be calling you from outside his room (for example, the library or away from campus), this can be a good idea. But remember the extra charge—this is more expensive than direct dialing but less expensive than collect.

Examine your own phone bill. You may be eligible for a discount plan based on the dollar amount of your calls to a particular area code. If you already participate in such a plan, think about whether you want to change the designated area code now that you have a child away at school. In some cases, setting up an "800" number at home might make sense depending on how many incoming long-distance calls you may have. Before opting for the "800" number, keep in mind that there will be a monthly service charge even during the summer months when your student is home.

"May I Ask Who's Calling?"

When the first phone call comes, the natural impulse is to send all the family members to the phone—at one time, on different extensions if possible. The conversation can be excited, somewhat stilted, and not very satisfactory. It's not unusual for the phone call from campus to begin with a plea for money. By the time you've dealt with the financial crisis, the younger siblings, if left to the end, feel slighted, and by that time your college youngster has to go anyway. Unless there is a reason for a three- (or four- or five- or six-) way conversation, you might be better off with separate calls.

What If the News Is Bad?

Phone conversations are often the worst way to hear—or deliver—bad news. Although your child has outgrown the "kiss it and make it better" stage of development, it's still true that being able to hug a youngster when he has a problem is often as reassuring as any words of advice you might offer. But now that he is off at school, phone calls will probably be your primary method of communication.

When your student calls with a problem, crisis, or major decision, often what he really needs more than anything else is a *good listener*. Parents hang up the phone upset, but frequently the student feels much better just having verbalized his feelings. You are his safety valve. Your role in the conversation may be reduced to uttering comforting phrases of "you're right," "uh-huh" or "that's normal," but in fact, that is *exactly* what your child needs to hear.

In any case, part of his college education is learning to think through a problem or a relationship and then to make a thoughtful decision. Even if he were living at home, this is the time that you would be stepping back from the decision-making process, while encouraging your child's independence and coping skills.

Unfortunately, parents sometimes also have to be the bearers of bad tidings. If you need to report an illness or death in the family, consider what you want your student to do *before* you call. If it's necessary to arrange an emergency trip home, have the information about suggested travel plans ready. If you really feel it unnecessary or unwise for your child to come home, be clear about your reasons. You might call the student's roommate, resident advisor, or dean of students and alert him to the problem if you feel that your youngster will need support and help coping with the news.

Sometimes a tragedy occurs involving one of your child's friends. While you may be hesitant to share the news, preferring not to reveal it until you can have a face-to-face conversation, remember that he is in touch with many of his friends from home who might unwittingly divulge the information.

You know your child best. Will he resent it if you choose to withhold information? Of course, you have to use your parental instincts in deciding when to tell the news. It's probably not wise to withhold bad news indefinitely, but timing is everything. News heard under stress can exacerbate the reaction. If your child is heading into five major exams, it's probably not the best day to tell him his pet died.

Don't be upset, however, or think your child is callous if he doesn't seem outwardly stricken by your news. He is in a different world now, with new and different pressures and perhaps less time to be buffeted by what is happening in his hometown. The news may bother you more than it bothers him.

It is not unusual, either, for a student to have a delayed reaction to bad news. One mother had to tell her daughter about the suicide of a best friend's parent. While the child seemed to take the news well, three weeks later, at midnight, there was a tearful three-hour phone call home about the need she still had in her life for *her* mother and the fears she harbored about losing her.

Often your student may not know what to do with the bad news you give him. He may have the best of intentions, but in the whirlwind of college life, he forgets the social niceties he practiced at home. If a condolence note is appropriate, remind your child to write one—even suggesting text if necessary. Suggest he phone or send a get-well card to a sick relative or friend.

THE WRITTEN WORD

"I never get anything in my mailbox."

"I wrote my daughter every day of her freshman year. It was probably too much, but she was so far from home and somehow it made me feel closer to chat about the day—just like when she was here."

After 18 years of living with him, you probably have a good idea of whether your child is a letter writer. If he is not, all the preaddressed envelopes or postcards are of little help. On the other hand, every college student likes to *receive* mail. Unlike a phone call, letters can be read—and reread—at leisure; amusing stories can be shared with the dorm.

Who are the letters for? You may find that writing to your child is a good antidote for your empty-nest feelings. But don't make your letters a litany of complaints or refer constantly to your own loneliness. This is not your student's responsibility.

Whether your child writes or not, letters from your end can be an important part of his new life. News about the little everyday happenings assures that when he arrives home, he knows what is going on and can more easily assume his place within the family. Even frequent phone conversations don't take the place of having something in his mailbox. As an alternative to a letter, try buying cards for special occasions, holidays, or just an "I-was-thinking-of-you" card.

On many campuses, mailboxes are not located within the dorm; it may be a hike to retrieve the mail. Because you may be the only person who writes to him consistently (most of his friends will probably communicate by phone or E-mail), if you plan to send something with a response deadline, it's wise to let him know by phone that it's coming so he can be sure to check his mailbox.

E-Mail, a Modern Variation on the Written Word

Many campuses are connected to Internet, an international computer network. While Internet provides many services and data banks, students seem to use it most to correspond with friends on other campuses. If you have a home computer and modem, you can access Internet, for a fee, through several on-line services such as Compu-Serve, America On-Line, and Prodigy. The postal service is cheaper, but if your student has E-mail on his computer in his room, he is more likely to check it regularly for messages—and perhaps more likely to correspond with you.

On the other hand, as one student told his mother via Internet, "Please still write to me. I like going to the post office and finding letters."

CARE PACKAGES

"I sent my son a batch of his favorite homemade cookies. To make sure he got them quickly I paid for overnight express delivery—but he didn't go to his mailbox until three days later."

"My daughter never called to thank me for the flowers I sent when she was sick—she thought they were from someone else."

When your child first gets to college he will probably ask you to send things he has just discovered he wants or that he may have forgotten. Even after that, every student welcomes a package, especially an unexpected one.

CHECK the college regulations for packages. Many schools have no provisions for direct delivery to dorm rooms. A welcome Care package can include things the student would have to replace at some inconvenience or cost to himself, particularly if the shopping center is not within easy walking distance from campus. But it doesn't have to include just necessities—unexpected treats are always a pleasant surprise. You might want to send business transactions like bank statements or phone bills separately to keep the package a fun experience.

Catalog shopping has made Care packages easier to send, but be sure to have a card enclosed indicating whom the goodies are from. Alternatively, check out the campus newspaper, directory, or personal contacts nearby for places that will fill telephone orders from you. Filling a box yourself (or with younger siblings) can also be fun—fun for you to assemble, fun for your child to receive, and certainly a very good way of keeping in touch.

Whatever the quality of food on campus, there will be times when your student will appreciate something to eat in his room, particularly if he has a refrigerator and/or microwave. Popcorn, nuts, fruit, packaged meals, noodles, or soups make nutritious convenience foods. Don't forget about boxes of cereal for the student who won't take time to go to a cafeteria for breakfast. Powdered-drink mixes (be sure to include a pitcher) can supplement carbonated soda.

You may question the need for sending groceries if your child could just as easily shop near campus for the same items— but as one student objected wistfully, "It's not the same as a Care package."

Aside from food, your student would always welcome that extra six-pack of socks for when he doesn't get the wash done. Underwear disappears, pantyhose runs, and cosmetics never last long enough. You can include toiletry samples that came in your own mail, and of course, tuck in some extra money (always appreciated) or even a gift certificate to a store near campus.

TIP: Rolls of quarters for washers and dryers always come in handy.

Help bridge the gap between high school and college by sending local news clippings, high school newspapers, family videos, pictures, and "mix" tapes from friends and siblings.

Don't forget to forward mail addressed to your student, and you can give a gentle hint about communication by enclosing stamped postcards addressed to family members.

For holidays like Halloween or Valentine's Day, you might want to send treats or decorations for the room. Packs of balloons, strings of lights, ribbons, stickers, and cardboard cutouts can make a dorm room seem a little more festive. Finish the theme off with paper goods like napkins and plates. You may also be able to provide your student with special attire for theme parties and dances.

One of the best Care packages can be an unscheduled (but not unannounced) visit from a traveling parent. Offers of dinner and even a good night's sleep as your guest at nearby lodgings can be very attractive. Call ahead and discuss your plans.

Birthdays at a Distance

Of course, one of the biggest holidays on your child's calendar will be his birthday. *Plan ahead.* You might want to find out the name of the food service or a nearby bakery that will deliver a decorated cake to campus—be sure to order in time. (At some schools, a club or student organization provides this service as a fund-raiser. If not, your student's resident advisor or an upperclassman can probably provide a list of area companies.)

While it might be fun to surprise your child, one family ruefully discovered the possible consequences. When they failed to tell their son about a cake they had ordered, he ignored a message on his door from the student organization that was trying to deliver it. Four days later, the parents found out that their son had never received the cake and that the student organization had already thrown out what was by then stale pastry. To add insult to injury, at the end of the month, the parents received a bill!

Check with your child's roommate(s) about plans for the day—if friends are giving a party or going to dinner, offer the cake as dessert or have your cake sent the preceding night. Be sure you allow enough leeway to have cards and packages arrive on the day.

One parent filled a "birthday" box with small, fun gifts, individually wrapped and labeled with instructions for when to open each. The celebration was carried out over several days, and although the total expense wasn't great, the student was overwhelmed—and wondered why he hadn't gone away for high school!

Exam Pick-Me-Ups

Another very popular time for sending Care packages is during reading period and exams. You may receive order forms from groups on campus or nearby stores. Check the list of what is to be included: If your student isn't likely to eat what is offered, assemble and send your own package of his favorites.

PARENTS' WEEKEND

"We don't spend this much time together when I'm home."
"I told my parents not to bother coming for Parents' Weekend, and then I was totally bummed out when they listened to me."

Most colleges sponsor an official Parents' Weekend. It's an opportunity to visit the school and see your child in his new environment. Frequently held in the fall, after students have been in classes for more than a month, the weekend usually includes seminars expressly for parents on a wide range of topics, concerts, receptions, and perhaps a football game (see Appendix I).

From the student's point of view, not only is it an opportunity to see the family, but it's also a chance to get some decent meals instead of the dormitory food they've been enduring (and complaining about).

To Go or Not to Go

If your child is at school some distance from home, the expense and time necessary for a weekend visit can be prohibitive. If he has recently been home on Fall Break, and with Thanksgiving just around the corner, you may question the need for a campus visit. Yet, especially for the first-year student, it's a wise investment, even if he seems nonchalant about having you there.

As with many things you do for your children, you won't necessarily "get credit" for attending Parents' Weekend, but you most certainly will "lose points" for not being there—especially if a roommate's family appears and you don't. Although parents can obviously visit campus on other weekends, Parents' Weekend has a special cachet. While a roommate's parents might include your child in some of their plans if you can't attend, your student may feel awkward or out of place under the circumstances.

These visits give the freshman an opportunity to show off. In just a short time he has become a member of a new community. This is his chance to share it with you. You can finally put faces to the names you've been hearing about in letters and calls.

TIP: Book your reservations early.

In many college towns, accommodations are limited, but even in larger metropolitan areas, good hotel/motel rooms close to campus go fast. Call the admissions office in the spring or summer *before* the start of school for the dates of the fall Parents' Weekend. (In some areas you can make reservations ahead for visits in succeeding years—and even for graduation!)

Remember that school doesn't stop for your child because you are there. Be sensitive to the academic and extracurricular demands on his time. That paper he didn't quite finish, or the exam the day after you leave, is a very real part of his new existence.

Extras That Make a Difference

A parent bearing gifts or offering services makes Parents' Weekend even more meaningful. Here are some suggestions:

- Bring any clothes or equipment he may have left behind; take the out-of-season wardrobe home with you.
- Now that your student has been on campus and scoped out the fashion trends, shop for needed additions.
- Offer to do his laundry.
- Shop for groceries for his room.
- Let him take a nap in your hotel room or stay with you, if he prefers.

SOME THOUGHTS BEFORE YOU GO

Before going to campus, ask yourself some questions about the kind of weekend you're anticipating—and talk to your child about what he is thinking.

1. Do you want to use this weekend as an opportunity to meet other parents? to get to know your child's roommate or resident advisor?

2. How does your student feel about doing things in groups? Will he want to go out with other parents and students?

3. How much time will your child be able to spend with you? Does he usually put Sunday aside as a workday, and how will he rearrange his schedule to include you? If you arrive earlier, what will you do while he is in class?

4. What are your options for off-campus eating? Your child is probably new to the area and may not know the restaurants well. Have him ask older students for recommendations, or check out guides, the local telephone directory, or other parents who may know.

Fantasy Versus Reality

Parents' Weekend can be like a brochure for a fancy resort—it sounds good until you get there. While both parents and student are anxious to see each other, Parents' Weekend may be the first time you are visiting your freshman on *his turf*.

The basic rule of thumb is to act as though you are a guest in someone's home. Resist the temptation to comment on, or clean, his dormitory room. Offer, only once, to do laundry, and drop the subject if your student seems offended. On the other hand, some families may resent doing laundry and chores during Parents' Weekend. It may be helpful to determine whether your child just wants the comfort and company or is really overwhelmed by housekeeping chores at school. If it's the latter, this is a good opportunity to help him develop strategies for coping.

Respect your child's need for privacy and independence, or else both sides may soon feel that they are spending more time together than they did during senior year of high school. Parents' Weekend is usually crammed with activities, but build in some time for the student to be alone with his friends. Allow time, away from the scheduled program, to walk and talk one-on-one. Your student may prefer to skip some of the activities and go off campus to shop, see a movie, and, of course, eat!

Should Sisters and Brothers Come Too?

Depending upon how you think your child is adjusting to school, you may or may not want to bring younger siblings with you to Parents' Weekend. Grabbing some private time to discuss any problems your freshman may be grappling with is more difficult with younger siblings around. Furthermore, while much of the weekend can be fun for all age groups, the seminars are usually geared specifically toward adults, and baby-sitters are difficult to find (unless you are going to ask your college student to baby-sit). Similarly, your college student may have difficulty knowing what to do on campus with a significantly younger brother or sister. Television or video games may not be readily available for entertainment. Think about what a younger child can do in a dorm room if your college student must study or accompanies you to a lecture. Teenage siblings will have an easier time fitting in.

On the other hand, Parents' Weekend usually finds the dormitory chock full of younger siblings sleeping on the floor and getting a taste of college life. For the younger brother or sister, it's a chance to reconnect with the college student. Be sure to discuss "the sibling factor" with your college student. He may have definite opinions one way or the other.

An Interesting Alternative

Some parents choose to use Parents' Weekend as a chance to spend quality one-on-one time with their college student away from campus. Some families figure the point of the weekend is to be with their child, and they decide to forego completely the football game/concerts/seminars, etc. Instead of staying on campus, they take their student on a minitrip away from school. Be sure to check whether this is something your child wants to do.

Postvisit Letdown

Like visitors' day at sleepaway camp, when the weekend visit is over, it's typical for parents and student to feel depressed. Sometimes Parents' Weekend, like other "command performances," can create anxiety for both sides. There is a great deal of trying to please one another. The weekend may not have fulfilled either the student's or the parents' (unrealistic) expectations. Uncontrollable things such as the weather can put a damper on planned activities, and when it's all over, even those freshmen who haven't experienced any real homesickness often find themselves feeling lonely when their parents have left and the hoopla is done. The best cure is to keep busy. Try to time your departure so that your student can be around friends or has an activity about to begin. Like any good "guest," send a note to your "host" telling him what a great time you had.

It's not easy to establish and maintain new lines of communication. There may be times when your child will insist upon privacy and will share very little of his experiences. But as with much of parenting, you just have to "hang in there." There is no simple solution. Even if the calls and letters seem to be primarily one-way, with you shouldering most of the burden of communication, maintaining the ties that bind is vitally important—in the long run—for the entire family.

Each family has to establish its own lines of communication. It's less a question of how often you hear from your child than how honestly and openly you talk when you do speak. Some students will share every detail of college life with their parents, while others tend to be more private. Either case is fine if you are sure that your child knows that he *can* tell you anything and everything if he so chooses. In the end, as one college senior explained, "What I really got out of all the calls and letters from home was the sense that there were always two people in this world who cared about me, no matter what."

LIFE GOES ON | 7

"It seemed that we had spent months focusing on my daughter's college experience. Her younger brother was just as excited as we were about the big move, and I guess I never took much time to think about what life would be like after she left. I figured we'd all take her, cry like everyone else said they did, come home, and pretty soon we'd all adjust and everything would be pretty much the way it had always been. On the way back from campus, we stopped for dinner, and as we waited for our food to arrive, we all looked at one another. The silence was deafening. I hadn't realized how much my daughter had carried the conversation."

When you find a really good book, you have conflicting emotions as you read it: you don't want to put it down, but you know that the more you read, the faster the end will come. Sending your child off to college brings contradictory feelings as well. On the one hand, you can't help but be caught up in the excitement of his new world, to say nothing of your sense of satisfaction at the job you've done from cradle to campus. But all the activity only seems to make time fly faster, and before you know it, you're back in your house starting another chapter. **Life on the homefront will be different**—and just as your student is adjusting to a new environment, so must you.

Despite the brave front you put on when you left him at school, by the time you get home, you may feel miserable. The house may seem empty, even if you still have younger children living there. You may find yourself walking *past* rather than *into* his abandoned room, even closing the door on it as though that will remove the reminder of earlier days. It seems odd to set the table with one less place—and, indeed, who inherits his chair and position?

Then again, you may be so excited by what is happening (or so mentally and physically exhausted) that there won't be any sense of loss at all until a while later in the year. Compounding the situation is the fact that the "mourning period" is not always the same length or time frame for everyone—and even though misery loves company, it doesn't always find it.

What are the manifestations of this change in your family? How can you ease the adjustment for yourself and the ones left at home? As adults, we've learned that for many of the problems in life, time is the great healer. The beginning may be rough because, despite the months of preparation, the actual goodbye is sudden. Then, the first time your child comes home, you realize that, "The more things change, the more they remain the same." The homefront is different, but it's still there.

THE OLD ORDER CHANGETH

"After our son and his friends left, my husband roamed the ball fields, looking for another team to fill his Saturday mornings."

"My son called his brothers after the first snowfall—noting that the sidewalks on campus had already been cleared, he mischievously asked who would be shoveling out the driveway at home."

By the time your student was a senior in high school, he could be (if he chose!) very helpful around the house. He may have been the one to mow the lawn or shovel the walk, do a last-minute grocery run, baby-sit "on call," drive carpool, or even assist with an elderly grandparent. By the time he leaves for college, you're not sure what you'll do without his help.

Perhaps he was your tutor-in-residence. One mother ruefully recounts calling her freshman at college for some long-distance help with his brother's seventh-grade math homework! Until you actually begin to live life without him, you probably won't appreciate how much time, perhaps even money, he saved you—and how many roles you are going to have to assume (or reassume!) in his absence.

From that standpoint, your days may well be busier than they were while your student was at home. On the other hand, his absence also leaves a void that you are going to have to fill. His companionship, his laughter, his outlook on the world, even his music—these are the things you have to replace. All those years of asking, "A little lower, please!" or "Do you have to run the water so long?"—now there may be an absence of noise, or at least it's at a lower decibel, and the water bills will probably be much smaller. One mother was surprised by how much she missed her daughter's friends coming in and out of her house; another noted that shopping trips just weren't the same. Still another sighed, "He's not the one of my three sons that I would have sent away!"

An Identity Crisis in the Making

Sending your child off to school often precipitates a mini- (or major) parental identity crisis. Who are you anyway? If you've always been referred to as "Johnny's mother" or "Sally's father," it's a jolt when you realize how many people don't even know your first name. Now that you're the parent of a college student, you may feel "older" ("Could I possibly be *that* old? Wasn't I just a student myself?"). You may worry about what role you will play in your student's life and be concerned that you are no longer needed. If you haven't worked outside the home, you may be anxious about how to fill your days. If you're employed, you may wonder whether the time you gave your child was enough to assure his continued bond with you. If your college student is an only child, the days may seem longer and lonelier now that he is away at school.

Of course, well-meaning friends don't help the situation by always observing, "Your house must feel empty now," "You must be very lonely," or "You must really miss him." One mother observed that if a family member had died, people wouldn't dwell on her loss every time they saw her.

There is no "right" answer for coping with your feelings of sadness, but there are a few do's and don't's to remember:

- **Do** build an adult relationship with your child by phone, letters, and Care packages (see Chapter 6); he'll let you know when "enough is enough."
- **Do** assess what you enjoyed doing before he left; if you did it because you like it and not just because of him, then continue.
- **Do** try to limit, if possible, any other major changes in your life for now; if you're going to move to a different house or neighborhood, prepare your child as far in advance as you can.
- **Do** keep your emotions under control; if you sob every time you speak with your child, you'll only make him feel guilty about leaving you.
- **Don't** burden him with uncertainties about your future; he's trying to figure out what he wants to do with his own life.
- **Don't** leap into commitments to substitute for the time spent with your college child; you may have had so much energy invested in him that you might want to focus for a while on other family members or yourself or even to change direction completely.
- **Don't** try to turn a sibling into a mirror image of the one who left; neither one of them will appreciate it.
- **Don't** wear your emotions for the other siblings to see; they may think the college child is more valued than they are.
- **Don't** feel guilty if you adjust to life without him more quickly than other parents do; everyone's situation will be different.

If you live close to campus, it's nice to be able to watch your student perform in a play or on the athletic field. On the other hand, if the school is at a distance from home, you can still be a part of these special events. Encourage your student (or one of his friends) to take pictures or even videotape the occasion.

Sometimes the campus newspaper covers an event: Ask for clippings and a print (offer to pay for the photograph and any mailing fees). The local town newspaper may also include college news and is a good resource for pictures.

If, despite all your best efforts, you're having a prolonged period of adjustment, seek professional help. One mother had an especially difficult time adjusting to her son's leaving. She cried often and became chronically depressed. A therapist helped her to recognize all the significant, serious changes she had endured in one year. Besides sending her son off to school, her mother had died and her husband had changed jobs during that same year. Sometimes the other things going on in your life may exaggerate the stress associated with leaving for college, and it's important (to you and your child) not to pin the blame on just that one event.

Common Signs of the (Parental) Freshman Blues

Looking back at some family pictures of her oldest son's freshman year, one mother laughed when she realized that the dreaded "freshman 15" hadn't been gained by her student, but had gone directly to her own hips. Weight gain—or loss—is common for parents of college freshmen. Some people eat when upset—others are turned off by food completely.

Increased marital tensions are common. You may argue more, snipe, or pick at one other. Your child used to be a buffer and sometimes an all-too-easy source of conversation material. Spouses may need to work on talking together again, perhaps even rediscover what they once had in common. Empty nesters can find the sounds of silence deafening. This period, said one father whose only child was in his freshman year, "was like the first few months of our marriage. It was learning—or actually relearning—how to live as a couple."

On the Other Hand

With one child off at school, there may actually be an easing of tensions at home, simply because you no longer have to juggle so many schedules. There will be more time to focus on yourself, your spouse, and your younger children. One mother laughed and said she never realized how delightful son number two was until she sent son number one off to school. "It was the first time he'd ever had a chance to shine on his own!"

For those with no kids now at home: While it's true that some couples find adjusting to the empty nest difficult, others, after a brief period of acclimation, enjoy the freedom of being a duo again. "We go to the movies when we want, eat what we want, and don't have to worry about who's at home when we're not!"

What to Do with His Room

"We hadn't even left the airport parking lot. I was in tears because I had just sent my older daughter off for her freshman year to a school halfway across the country. From the back seat comes this little voice wanting to know, 'Can I have Rachel's room?'"

Ideally, you will leave the freshman's room at home intact— at least until after his first visit home. There is a sense of continuity, familiarity, and belonging he will get by returning to find his things still in place. You don't want him to feel that he's been replaced or that he's just a visitor in his home. It's doubtful that you'll take seriously the suggestion of one little girl who wanted to turn her brother's room into a private Nintendo arcade.

On the other hand, some families have had to play musical rooms before this, and it won't be such a dramatic shift in thinking if there's another move now. Realistically, too, if your other children have been sharing a room, having one remain empty for months at a time can be a source of very visible irritation to them. You might also want to use that room for grandparents or out-of-town visitors instead of juggling things around when they come. There are certainly valid reasons for dispossessing the college student on either a temporary or permanent basis, but before you do:

- Get his input on the changes you want to make—before you make them.
- If he's to give up his room, let him move some of the furnishings as well.

- If he's to share his room, be sure that the new "roommate" respects his possessions while he's away and that you set out some rules for peaceful coexistence when he's home.
- When guests use his room on a temporary basis, check to see that things are left as he had them.
- Don't forget to allow for privacy when he comes home. It's what he may crave more than anything since there's precious little of it in dorm living.

TIP: Don't assume that younger siblings will want to switch rooms. They may want to keep this vestige of "the way things used to be."

THE SUBJECT IS SIBLINGS

"My three-year-old hadn't seen her brother in so long that when she heard he was coming home for Thanksgiving, she solemnly responded, 'I thought he died.'"

"I'll be glad when he goes back to school so that I can assume my rightful place at the head of the table." (Comment by younger brother during Fall Break)

When a child leaves for college, parents aren't the only ones left behind. Siblings can be just as tearful, just as excited, and just as lonely. Some will rush to the phone when it rings, eager to share their latest news or ask for advice; others will write regularly—and expect an immediate reply. One little girl kept the light on in her sister's room at night—so she could pretend that someone was still there.

If the cost is not prohibitive, you might want to put up with regular telephone calls, initiated by the child at home, until he adjusts to life without his older sibling. Try not to limit his conversation, which is very important to him, to the end of one of your phone calls. Younger children enjoy putting Care packages together and, of course, receiving something in return. Wearing T-shirts, hats, or sweatshirts with the college logo sets up another bond with campus—and they're even more prized when sent by the older sibling.

Depending on his age, a sibling can stay in the dorm when you're visiting campus or even travel there himself during school vacations. In fact, siblings may well come to view the entire college move as an exciting adventure, bringing with it all sorts of opportunities they had never imagined. If there is an age gap, there may even be a certain amount of boasting to friends about this older sibling who has gone off to some strange place called college. On the other hand, some siblings may envy the college student's life and independence or the parental attention bestowed on each call from campus or visit home. Whatever the initial reaction, the fact that younger brothers and sisters will be in school themselves usually helps them resume their own lives without a lengthy period of adjustment.

Beyond any of these emotions, however, the oldest sibling left behind faces a change in his family position. The buffer is gone, and now he moves up a notch: *He's* the oldest. Whether he wants them or not, he may have more responsibilities at home and will certainly be a greater focus of attention than he was before. From the sibling's viewpoint, the extra attention may not be welcome. As one younger sister complained, "I don't want to have dinner with you all the time!"

Sometimes the "new oldest child" can't win. Whatever good qualities his sibling had, he is expected to emulate; whatever his sibling lacked, he is expected to make up for. Rather than pattern one after the other, encourage the younger child to develop different interests (unless he is clearly as talented in the same area). If the first child was not as successful as you would have hoped, avoid the temptation to do things "the right way" the second time. The younger child will be caught in the middle.

When Younger Siblings Visit

There are many reasons for younger brothers and sisters to visit their college sibling at school, not the least of which is the fun both visitor and freshman have. Some colleges even sponsor "sibling weekends." For the younger child, it's an opportunity to experience college life. It's also a chance to establish a different, more mature relationship with his sibling, outside the boundaries of the family home and without parental input. The college student will enjoy showing off his new environment and friends.

But before anyone packs any bags, the two of them should talk about, and plan, the visit—what the younger child wants to do while he's there, how long he'll be on his own, and how he'll spend that time. It's also wise to remind both the guest and the host of some important ground rules:

- *NO DRINKING.* No matter what decision your college student has made about alcohol consumption for himself, it's important to stress that you expect the younger sibling not to imbibe. Warn against drinking any punch or opened cans of soda at parties—you don't know what's been added.
- *Choose parties wisely.* Part of the excitement of the visit is to go to a college party. Suggest that they go early and stay only a short while before drinking and behavior get out of hand.
- *Keep the visit short.* Two nights is more than enough for both siblings. Dorm rooms are short on space, and the college student has classes and coursework to concentrate on.

Having said this, however, it should be noted that you realistically have no control over what's happening when you send a younger child to visit. As one freshman advised, "Cross your fingers and think about something else. The older sibling won't let you down—but if he does, you'll never know about it."

HOW'S HE DOING?

"My daughter had always been a terrific writer, but she got a C on her first college paper."

"I thought that because I was paying his tuition, I'd at least see his grades—wrong!"

Because your child doesn't come home every day, you won't be privy to much of what goes on at school. You'll have his address and phone number, maybe a schedule of his courses, and often a healthy dose of anxiety about how he's spending his time. Everything you've read and heard makes it obvious that college life isn't the same as when you were 18. Social and academic issues, along with questions about your child's future after college, are legitimate concerns. The bottom line, though, is that you're not there. You can offer advice and support, but however much you talk on the phone or write letters, in the end you're going to have to trust your child to do the "right" thing—even when his "right" is not yours.

Those First Grades

Your student's mark on his first college paper or midterm may be consistent with his high school record, but for many freshmen—and their parents—those grades are a real shock.

NOTE: Grades are mailed—and addressed—to the student either at home or at school; some colleges offer the option of sending a copy to the parents.

Classes at college are tougher than the ones in high school, and some are more demanding than others. Lower grades may simply be a reflection of stiffer requirements and evaluation than your child expected. Even the best students can find that their grade point averages decline during freshman year.

Often, the many distractions on campus eventually impact on grades. Without a parent there to remind a child of deadlines and without strong personal study habits, it can be easy to falter. College professors assume that everyone takes responsibility for keeping up with the reading, but without the regular checks of high school, things can slide until a student finds himself overwhelmed at exam time.

It's especially difficult for students who come to school with a set course of study, particularly premed, in mind and find that they either don't like it or don't have an ability in the field. Then they feel as if they're failing (or faring poorly) in more than just a single course. These emotions are compounded when a student believes he is not living up to *your* expectations of him because *you* expect him to be a doctor, lawyer, or engineer. It's even more problematic if he's attending a specialized school or division (such as a tech or engineering program) where it is difficult to transfer credits or choose another major.

Set Realistic Expectations

Talk candidly with your student about his grades—preferably nonjudgmentally—and set realistic expectations for him. If something goes wrong academically, find out the reason and offer suggestions. If it's simply a matter of not realizing how much work his courses really demand, you may have to be patient while he learns to budget his time and set priorities. Suggest that he study in the library to cut down on distractions in the dorm and that, when given a choice, he take the more rigorous courses later in his college career.

Your child may flounder because he chose a course too difficult for him or because one of his required courses is in an area he was never good at. Generally, too, there is a higher reading load, more term papers are required, and there is a more rigorous examination of the research a student presents. A college class may be the first time that a student will do independent research using primary sources. The school itself provides a support structure to help, but the first step has to be the student's. He must recognize that he needs help—preferably early in the semester. Professors and teaching assistants hold regular office hours, whether for a lecture class or a small seminar. Although it may seem obvious to you, emphasize to your student that *it is the professor's job* to teach the subject and to connect with students. Seeking additional help is not an intrusion or burden.

Most schools also assign each student an academic advisor. Again, encourage your child to be honest with himself—and his advisor—if he is in trouble. The academic advisor or professor can suggest a tutor (frequently a graduate student) if necessary.

Suppose He Fails?

If a student is realistic about his performance early in the semester, he may decide to drop a course rather than risk a failing grade. Explore the possibility of taking a difficult course during the summer, even at a local college, and then transferring the credit. One student, struggling with a required statistics course her freshman year, dropped the class, opting to take it at night at her local college during the summer. Without the pressures of four other classes, she was able to focus on and pass the course. If your child decides to go this route, however, be sure he gets academic approval from the college where he is matriculating before registering elsewhere. Some schools will not accept credit from the college that may be closest to your home.

It's tough for your child to go into a new environment, forced to confront his own strengths and weaknesses. If he's having academic trouble, you may have to bolster his self-confidence. **REMEMBER: Reassure him that he does indeed belong there, and that the college knew what it was doing when it accepted him.**

When your student's marks suffer from an overactive social life, it's frustrating and not easy to be so understanding. You should certainly talk seriously to him (without lecturing) about your expectations, and disappointments, as well as to remind him how much his education is costing your family. You might suggest that he prioritize what he's doing and not put academics at the very bottom of his list!

You know your child best, and how long you are willing to be patient with him is going to be an individual decision. Some parents send their students off to college with that old adage, "I don't pay for Cs." Before using financial clout, however, be absolutely sure that partying really is the reason for the low marks. Your child's socializing may be a frustrated explosion because he is in over his head academically. Remember, too, the rule you lived by when he was a toddler: Don't make a threat you don't intend to follow through on.

RELIGION ON CAMPUS

"Our son went back to attending services after he started dating the lead singer in the church choir."

"My daughter completed two courses in comparative religions—and announced she'd be traveling to third-world holy sites over the summer rather than taking a job that would earn her money for next year's expenses."

Because college years are a time of experimentation and examination, don't be surprised if your child starts questioning long-held religious beliefs. It's not unusual for a student to declare he's become more—or less—religious. He may

CULTS ON CAMPUS

Religious cults are a rare but genuine threat to college students. Homesickness and anxiety about college life and academics can make a student especially vulnerable.

If you are genuinely concerned that your student has gotten involved with a religious cult, it's especially important to keep open your lines of communication with your child.

1. Check with the college administration to see whether the organization is sanctioned as a recognized student activity and register a complaint about its activities.

2. Consult with your local clergy for background information on the group. Consider joining a support group of parents whose children have joined cults. It's important not to feel isolated.

3. Do not condemn or insult your student about his involvement in the group; this will only alienate your child further, something that works to the cult's advantage.

announce that he is an agnostic or an atheist—or that he has changed religions completely, possibly to an established faith, possibly to a group with whom you are unfamiliar.

Remember that college may offer your student the opportunity to explore a wide variety of practices and beliefs. He may be meeting individuals of another faith for the first time. One freshman was honest when she met her roommate and admitted that she had never met anyone Jewish before.

In addition, the social component of a particular religious group on campus may be especially inviting. Your child may choose to join a group because his friends are active in the organization. One student who steadfastly refused to go to church during his senior year in high school surprised his parents by becoming very involved in his college Newman Club. It was a large group, offering a variety of interesting activities and social action programs, led by a strong, friendly campus advisor.

What should you do if your child chooses a religious path different from the one in which you raised him?

- Give it time. This may be a phase, even a challenge to see your reaction.
- Keep the lines of communication open. You *want* to find out what he finds compelling about his new beliefs.
- Respect his choices. As with much of college, it may not be your preference, but ultimately it is his decision to make.

LOVE BLOOMS—AND WITHERS—ON CAMPUS

"My parting words to my daughter were, 'Don't fall in love freshman year.' We'd been home barely two days when she called to tell us that she had met the man she wanted to marry!"

"This is not a dating campus. It's either random hookups or a serious relationship."

In many ways, campus romance today is a long way from the dating scene of the fifties, even the sixties. There's not much of the "I'll call you Wednesday for a date Saturday night," and the idea of the male paying for the evening is generally an obsolete concept. It's more likely that your student, instead of having a "girlfriend" or "boyfriend," will have many more *friends* of the opposite sex; that he will socialize in large, mixed groups; and that when he does get involved, it will quickly become more intense. Campus courtship can be a matter of days (and nights).

On the other hand, star-crossed (and not) lovers do find each other on campus and romance does flourish.

Saturday Nights and Through the Week

Dating on campus isn't limited to weekends. You can meet for breakfast, lunch, or dinner; before, after, and in class; or for a myriad of activities and programs—or for nothing at all— every day of the week. Some students do limit social life to the weekend, reserving the weeknights for study, but others deliberately study together throughout the week. In fact, more than a few happy couples trace the beginning of their romance to struggling through calculus together.

On the down side, a freshman can find himself involved exclusively with one person almost before he knows it, and certainly before he has a chance to make many other new friends at school. You might not know who she is, and she may not be the person *you* would have chosen for him!

The campus love interest who lives within a few hours of where you live can even monopolize your child's time when he's home for vacation to the point that you almost feel that she's already a member of the family. His old high school friends might cross him off their list because he's never free to be with them. You may resent the situation (silently or not so silently), wring your hands about the mistake he's making, and hint about the folly of leaping too early—but you'll soon realize that whatever you do while he's at home, he has all that time on campus to do as *he* pleases. In fact, on the chance that this is "for real," be sure to avoid personal attacks that will sour any future relationship you will have with him. Gaining a daughter is better than losing a son, and vice versa.

The love interest of the 18-year-old may not last, but the short-term intensity and the fact that they may still have to see each other frequently can make the breakup that much more painful. If you've been able to maintain close ties with your child, despite your feelings about his romance, those lonely, disconsolate phone calls are sure to follow.

When he was a toddler, you could kiss a scraped knee and make the pain go away like magic, but you can't do that now. You can only offer a comforting shoulder (perhaps heave an inward sigh of relief) and encourage him to get very busy. Resist the temptation to say, "I told you so," or run down the relationship in which he invested so much time. If you think he's having problems dealing with the situation, encourage him to talk about his feelings with a counselor; if his grades are suffering, suggest that he get some extra academic help.

Of course, if your student attends a single-sex college or one where the male-female ratio is lopsided, the social life tends to center around the weekends. In those circumstances, as one upperclassman explained, "road tripping is a must." Students at all-women colleges tend to leave campus on weekends for a social life at other schools, while all-male colleges are transformed when Friday rolls around.

Date Rape

This is an increasingly explosive issue on campus with emotional, and legal, ramifications for men and women. Some research suggests that one out of five female college students will be the victim of a completed or attempted rape by someone she knows. Drugs and alcohol are frequently involved in rape cases, and a recent study reports that 90 percent of all reported campus rapes occurred when the assailant, the victim, or both had been drinking.

To deal with this frightening problem, some colleges have detailed codes of conduct that require clear consent before proceeding with any physical contact, from casual kissing to sexual intimacy (see Appendix F). The issue is so fraught with emotion, on both sides, that accusations initiated at on-campus judicial hearings have been carried over into the off-campus court system.

NOTE: Rules governing campus judiciary proceedings may not be the same as those for civil or criminal court.

Whatever the verdict about intent, however, the action itself can leave long-term emotional scars. Caution your daughter to make sexual intentions clear (no mixed messages) and to avoid obviously potentially dangerous situations:

- If the drinking is getting out of hand, leave.
- When you go to parties, establish a buddy system with a female friend who agrees to watch where you go and with whom.
- If your date is drunk, go home with a female friend.
- Don't drink to excess, but if you think you've had too much to drink, leave with a female friend. Don't go to your date's room. Never take a nap to "sleep it off" in an empty room of a party house. Go back to your own dorm with a female friend or call a resident advisor or campus security to help you. (At some colleges, however, the local police serve as campus security, so your underage student may face legal problems because of drinking.)
- Avoid drinking punch or from an open can—you can't be sure what has been added to the mixture.
- Don't leave your dorm room unlocked.

- Don't invite any man to your room or go to his room when you are alone unless you know there are other people on the dorm floor you can call for help.
- Don't argue with your date if you've said "no" and your date continues to press the point or suggests that the two of you can just talk. Leave the room and immediately seek other people.
- Tell a resident advisor or other campus authorities if a date physically or emotionally harasses you.

The question of date rape is frequently discussed during freshman orientation. Men sometimes feel like battle lines are being drawn. One freshman remarked that a lecture on date rape was "a session of male-bashing. I was angry that the general assumption was that men were out of control and couldn't be trusted."

Make clear to your son that there is **no** room for ambiguity in any sexual relationship. A "no" is a "no" even if accompanied by a giggle. **Both** partners must clearly want to proceed at each stage of a sexual relationship.

. . . and Sexual Harassment

Communication between the sexes is still a problem. Be sure that your student reads and understands the college regulations about sexual harassment, rights, responsibility, and means of redress (see Appendix F).

Men need to understand that there is a strong political climate on most campuses that will not tolerate any form of harassment. This includes any unwanted verbal, nonverbal, or physical sexual contact. It can also refer to obscene gestures, sexual insults (gay or straight), jokes, questions, suggestions, offensive pictures—anything that adversely affects the working or learning environment of an individual. What in another age might have been construed as typical banter or swagger is generally unacceptable today.

Even a chance comment or an expression of anger can be construed as sexual harassment and the subject of a grievance. In one nationally reported instance, a foreign student yelled in his native language at a group of noisy women, calling them "water buffaloes." He was brought up on disciplinary charges, although the case was eventually dismissed.

Colleges now have formal grievance procedures to report any case of sexual harassment by a professor, teaching assistant, resident assistant, or university administrator. Stress that your student should never feel compromised or threatened, either physically or emotionally, by a professor or someone representing the college. Using grades or the promise of special treatment in exchange for sexual favors is illegal. While schools are committed to academic freedom, there is no room in the classroom for derogatory or demeaning remarks about gender, sexual orientation, or ethnic or minority groups. Report any such instances to the appropriate campus authority.

Gays on Campus

As in society in general, there are gays and lesbians on every campus. Some colleges have a very strong gay and lesbian student community, while at others, homosexuals are still very much in the closet. A quick glance at the campus bulletin boards and college newspaper will tell you about the public profile and activities of the local gay population. In any case, your student may be exposed to information, situations, and pressures he hasn't previously encountered.

While young people may have nervously joked about the issue, this is the time for a serious discussion about sexual preferences, personal values, and tolerance. It's especially important to keep the lines of communication open about this subject because your student may need to talk to you but worry what your reaction will be if he brings up the subject.

One freshman at a small midwestern college found himself in an uncomfortable situation. He was sitting in the dorm lounge watching television when an upperclassman he knew only casually joined him. At first the conversation was general in tone, but after about 15 minutes the freshman became uncomfortable when he suddenly realized that the older student seemed to be making a pass at him. After a hasty exit, the freshman returned to his room confused and worried. Was it something he did? Did he misread the signals from the beginning? Did others think he was gay? Was he, in fact, gay and didn't know it—otherwise, why was he being approached by a gay student? It's important to reassure your child that his sexuality is not determined by who is attracted to him, nor does it say anything about his own sexuality if any of his friends are gay.

Maintaining an open line of communication permits your child to talk to you about these serious issues. Whether the conversation is about his own sexual orientation or about gay issues in general, it's important that your child feels comfortable discussing these critical concerns with you.

If Your Child is Gay

The college years are frequently a time for coming to terms with one's sexual orientation. For many students, it is during late adolescence that they have their first intimate sexual experience (either heterosexual or homosexual).

If your student is gay, parent-child communication is all the more important. Whatever your religious, moral, or personal beliefs about the gay life experience, you need to talk openly, honestly, *and respectfully* about his decision. You need to have the same conversations about sexual issues that you would have with a heterosexually active young adult. You must stress the need to practice safe sex.

If you are having trouble accepting your child's gay lifestyle, talk to a member of the clergy or seek out local parent support groups. You may—or may not—approve of his choice, but he remains your child. He needs your nonjudgmental love and support, perhaps now more than ever.

Hopefully, your child has chosen a campus where a homosexual lifestyle is readily accepted. If not, remind him that sexual harassment is illegal and that he need not tolerate acts of bias or hate. However, realistically, he may choose to transfer to a school that is more diverse and accepting.

GREEK LIFE ON CAMPUS

"My son's fraternity raised thousands of dollars for the local children's hospital."

"My son chose his college in part because it had a strong Greek system—and then he didn't get a bid from the fraternity he wanted to pledge."

When your child applied to his college, you may not have paid much attention (even if *he* did) to the presence or absence of fraternities or sororities. Now that he's a freshman, you may hear a great deal more if his campus officially recognizes them or even if they exist off campus unofficially. What should you expect if your child decides to join?

To Join or Not to Join?

As with most anything else that is going to happen during this year, the news is neither all good nor all bad. On the plus side, Greek life offers a ready-made group of friends, who have an active, planned social life and usually a commitment to social action projects on and/or off campus.

In those schools with housing facilities for fraternities and sororities, your bill for room and board may actually be lower (although dues will be an added expense). One mother noticed that it cost less for her son to live in his fraternity house than in the dorm and that the food was significantly better. Your child may also save money on entertainment because Greek organizations sponsor activities and social functions almost every weekend. Joining a particular fraternity or sorority may even be a tradition in your family, and it does provide another outlet for networking when your student enters the work force.

On the other hand, becoming a member is a time-consuming process of parties and activities, often at the beginning of the school year. There is surely a certain amount of social casting involved as freshmen try to fit into a group that looks and behaves the way they do. As a parent, your knowledge of Greek life may be limited to the movie *Animal House* and newspaper stories of hazing atrocities. Fraternities are often cited as places where alcohol is rampant, sex is more than a fact of life, and public property is destroyed. The national Hellenic organizations do have the power to oversee individual chapters and place them on probation or even suspend them, but college administrators are still concerned about the abuses leading up to that discipline. Of course, it's also true that this kind of lifestyle isn't restricted to campuses where a Greek system is in place.

Making the Decision

Regardless of how you feel, this is another one of those freshman decisions that probably won't be yours to make. It's tempting for parents, especially of students on largely "Greek campuses," to equate social acceptance with membership in a fraternity or sorority, perhaps even a specific one. There's a certain sigh of relief that he's "made it," that he has friends and is somehow part of campus life.

Sometimes this can mean more to you, though, than it does to your child. He may not feel comfortable with the day-to-day demands of a lifestyle that might look so appealing from a distance. A quiet or shy child may even be reluctant to socialize at the opening parties, and even if he does, he may not spark the quick good impression necessary to be accepted. If he wants to try, give him whatever encouragement he needs, but don't set up false expectations about a situation you may know little—if anything—about.

Of course, if you belonged to a fraternity or sorority, and your child has grown up with that familiarity, you've already influenced his decision. But don't assume that the chapter on his campus will be the same as yours was. The character can change with the membership, even from campus to campus, and he's going to choose the one whose members are most compatible with him.

Although your child probably won't be calling for permission or advice about joining, you may receive sad phone calls if he is rejected. The fact is, however, that you may still be mourning about the turn of events when his next—happy—call comes. Youth is usually resilient—and, besides, most of the parties are open.

WHAT DO THEY DO FOR FUN?

"We sat out on the lawn until four in the morning just talking."
"For Halloween, the whole campus got dressed up in costumes, even the president of the college."

College life is more than classes and studying—it should be. As the year progresses, you may hear details of what your student is doing, but more likely, you'll hear snatches of "news reports" on campus activities. So what do they do?

Party Time

Parties, large and small, are one of the main forms of campus socializing. Generally, dates are not required, and people are welcome to attend solo or with friends.

REMEMBER: Alcohol is generally abundantly available at campus parties. Talk to your student about how he will handle these social situations.

Remind him that underage drinking may be dealt with on campus as a disciplinary problem, but that if he is arrested for it (either on or off campus), he may have a criminal record when he graduates. Indeed, more and more colleges are revising, and tightening, their alcohol policy. As one administrator told students, "I can't tell you how to live, but I am the person who calls your mother when you get killed."

Sports

Sports of all sorts can generally be found on most campuses. Besides the varsity level of play, there may be a wide range of club and intramural programs, as well as plenty of pickup games. Even the athletically inept often have a spot on the team. Encourage your student to participate—it's fun, good exercise, and a way to meet new people.

Clubs and Activities

Most schools offer a wide range of clubs and activities— enough to keep participants busy and involved. It's a fun way to meet other students, offers a way to contribute to the community, and can even help develop significant job skills. Some activities, such as the campus newspaper and drama productions, can be very demanding, almost like a full-time job. Remind your student that academics are his first priority, no matter how interesting the organization.

Plays, Movies, Lectures, Exhibits, Bands

Colleges offer a myriad of programs—lectures, plays, and so on—on campus weekly and sometimes daily at affordable prices, if not for free. Your student will find plenty to keep him busy. The more remote campuses bring in visiting artists, speakers, and musicians, while the more urban schools also draw on the surrounding area.

And Nothing at All

Some of the fun on campus is what we would describe as "nothing at all"—the delight of having a large group of peers readily available. The student center or local campus hangout are integral parts of the college social life. Whether schmoozing, snacking, or at impromptu pizza parties, you can always find someone who wants to talk, at any hour of the day. That is one of the secret treasures of campus life.

SHUTTLING BACK AND FORTH?

"The higher the tuition, the fewer the number of days they will be in class."
"My daughter brought her beach clothes back to school after Winter Break so that she didn't have to spend time shopping before her island vacation over Spring Break."

Your child may have left in August, but he can be back again almost before you unpack your bags, whether for a quick weekend visit from a nearby school or on a scheduled school holiday.

To Come Home or Not to Come Home?

College academic schedules are just not what they were when you were in school. Even a two-day school break can stretch out to a week if your child has no classes the day before or after it, and you'll surely be asked by at least one friend, "Is he off again?!"

How often—and whether—he actually comes home during these school minibreaks will depend partly on finances, his new life, and your own plans now that he is away. When you check his calendar and see that he has a break, it's easy enough for a freshman parent to assume that, distance and budget permitting, he'll want to come home—but that's not always the case. In fact, there can be an emotional tug of war between the student who is trying to settle in to all of the expectations and realities of his first year and the parent on the homefront who hasn't yet given up the high school senior.

TIP: Don't make an assumption without discussion.

You'll probably find that he will be eager to come home early in the year before he becomes used to his new life, if only to touch base with his old friends and the room he left behind. As the year goes on, however, he may announce plans to visit a roommate, college friend, or even an old high school chum on another campus. It's tough to share your child with people you don't really know yet, but enticing him home by way of a guilt trip is only going to postpone his inevitable separation from you.

There's a fine line between letting him know that you would love to see him and making him feel miserable if he follows an urge to go elsewhere. It's tough for anyone to deal with dead silence or a choked-back sob after announcing intentions to go somewhere else. On the other hand, after one mother encouraged her son several times to accept an invitation to a friend's beach house for Spring Break, he finally asked whether she would prefer that he never come home at all.

Be honest—and realistic—about your feelings from the beginning. It's probably unwise to pressure your child to spend all his off days at home, but you can certainly convey to him which are the most important ones. If he doesn't want to come home when you had planned, suggest an alternate date or consider visiting campus yourself when his schedule permits. His refusal to come home may have nothing to do with you and everything to do with all the options his new world has opened for him. If you're planning a family vacation around one of his holidays, he may also want to join you more readily if he thinks that he will be the only one of his old friends to be home—or if he likes your vacation choice! Realize, too, however, that if he is playing on a sports team or otherwise immersed in a college

TIPS FOR LONG-DISTANCE TRAVEL

1. Schedule airline travel as early as possible. Discount fares, special student fares, and frequent-flyer seats sell out quickly, especially around college breaks.

2. When making an airline reservation, take note of restrictions and be sure you can make changes in case your child cannot meet his original plans.

3. Keep a record of the airline ticket number (even if your child makes the reservation) in case the ticket is lost or misplaced.

4. Confirm travel 48 hours prior to departure.

5. If your child is traveling by train, try to get seat reservations beforehand.

6. Have an alternate route in case of emergency, particularly at peak holiday times.

7. Check for any further travel update before leaving home or campus—newscasts always seem to feature college students stranded at airports.

activity, he may have to stay on campus even when classes are out.

Whatever your emotions about seeing your child during his breaks, his decision to go elsewhere has financial implications as well. Who will pay? Absorbing the cost of his travel home is one thing, but how do you feel about funding a vacation? Even if he uses his own money, it means he has that much less for his on-campus expenses. One father wondered whether his daughter's fun in the sun was supposed to give him vicarious enjoyment while he put in ten-hour days at the office to pay for her tuition.

If you can laugh about the situation, fine—some parents really enjoy sharing the excitement from afar and can afford to encourage their children's travels. But if you resent the expense, be honest in the beginning; don't supply the funds and then dwell on the expenditure for months afterward. The cost of coming home may, in fact, balance the cost of going elsewhere (or, in the case of colleges at a distance, exceed it)—and you'll have to decide whether to use the power you have over the purse strings.

Suppose He Can't Come

There can be so many breaks in the academic calendar that distance, budget, and your own schedule may preclude your student from coming home for all of them. One parent was surprised to learn that her daughter had a full week off in October. Because the girl was attending school almost a thousand miles from home and was on need-based financial aid, it was impossible for her to afford an additional trip. She and her parent contacted the head of residential life to be reassured that campus was a viable (and lively) alternative chosen by many students.

Staying at school during a break is usually not a lonely experience. Some colleges plan for this and provide trips to nearby places of interest or even special dinners. Local alumni may also be recruited to ease a child's time away from family.

Creative planning of trips by family members can offset a feeling of separation at holiday times. A business executive was able to visit his two college students (on different campuses) before and after long holiday weekends. Some families will plan an excursion to their student's college town for shorter breaks. One mother was happy to see how excited her daughter was at the thought of just "crashing" in a hotel with her family for a weekend. She savored the hot shower, the room service, and the "quiet" of the hotel room. The parents realized that their student didn't need to travel home to feel the closeness of her family.

REMEMBER: Vacation times with a college student do not *always* have to revolve around his schedule.

Your work and home routine and that of younger and older siblings should prove just as important.

When it is apparent that your child won't be able to share Thanksgiving, a birthday, or a religious observance with you at home, talk honestly and openly about his plans. "I'll wing it," may be his response when you ask what he will be doing—

but that's not good enough! You should have a clear idea of what and with whom he will be spending the time.

Although he may not miss coming home, at least in theory, when the holiday arrives and he's miles from home, he may be hit with an unexpected case of the blues. Telephone calls help; Care packages are always welcome.

Dealing with His Absence

You, celebrating at a distance, may also be having mixed feelings about the absence of your college student at holiday times. Was it the right thing to do, letting him go so far away? Should we have put aside some additional funds for extra travel expenses? Emotional as you may be at these times, it is not a good idea to second-guess your decision.

Instead, acknowledge your feelings of loss—and those of siblings too—but then be realistic about changes in your family. Now that you've made arrangements for your college student, enjoy the holidays yourself. You may even want to make different arrangements for celebrating that would be more suitable—and perhaps more exciting—for your smaller family.

If a relative lives near your child's college, holiday plans can be eased. The choice to attend a school at a distance may even have included the presence of an important family member close to that particular campus. This gives your child a true sense of an extended family and leads to a closeness that is mutually satisfying. From your standpoint, a relative is a person who can give you a true account of how your student looks and how he is doing.

WELCOME HOME!

"'Mom, don't buy the tree until I get home!' It sounded good, but I knew if I waited, all the good Christmas trees would be gone."

"I couldn't deal with hearing the front door bang in the wee hours of the morning any more. I was tempted to build a separate side entrance for her."

You'll soon realize that the emotional goodbye on campus really didn't signal a cataclysmic break with the family. Daily living may change, but basic personalities and relationships remain the same—perhaps to the dismay of some who share the sigh of one little sister, "But I thought he would have gotten nicer while he was away!"

Through the Front Door and . . .

That first visit back home! You've prepared the house (and yourself) as though you're having an important guest. Your child's room is neat and clean, pillows have been fluffed (and refluffed), favorite foods are in the refrigerator, and now you're even a little nervous with anticipation. How will he look? How will you look to him? How much has he changed?

Then the door opens, and he arrives, disheveled and exhausted, perhaps looking through you or beyond you, as uncertain about what to expect as you were. You have a million questions, but he hasn't had to answer personal questions every day—nor has he been required to hug someone morning or night.

Initial joy on your part soon becomes tempered with the reality of your child's new lifestyle. His biological clock is so irregular that he sleeps during the day and is up (making noise) or just going out when you're on your way to bed. You may have had some sleepless nights the summer before he left for college—now they're back again, or perhaps just starting. The phone rings at all hours, the bill is up, and there's no more hot water in the bathroom. The stereo and TV are blaring, half-made sandwiches are left on the counter, and you can't find a clean glass anywhere. He's b-a-a-ck!

Your child's arrival home can be just as difficult for him. No one has been questioning his hours or his cleanliness. His friends have come and gone into his dorm as they pleased, and he certainly hasn't had to drive anyone to music lessons. As a matter of fact, he's probably made more decisions in a shorter period of time than he will make later in life. Being on campus is a different world. He has gotten a taste of complete independence—and it's going to be tough to take the spoon out of his mouth now.

On the one hand, you've missed your child while he's been away and you've been looking forward to a new, adult relationship with him. On the other hand, it's easy to resent the different set of house rules that may be established for his visit—and to feel guilty about your resentment.

It all comes down to a question of turf and courtesy. When you visit him on campus, it's his turf, and you have to respect it; when he's home, it's family turf, and both sides are going to have to communicate and compromise. If you're too strict about the rules, your child may use them as an excuse to stay away or visit friends on future vacations. If you take a complete hands-off approach and allow him total freedom so that he drops by only to change clothes or get some spending money, it's certainly not going to be a very satisfactory visit from your standpoint, to say nothing of the complaints it's likely to spark in younger siblings.

Some of the Issues

Life with the college student may not run as smoothly as you had hoped. Things you used to argue about can still be sources of friction, and there will be new ones as well.

Laundry and household chores. When he was living at home, you may have had a tacit agreement that the door would be closed on his messy room. Now that he's away, it's been cleaned out and you've gotten used to the uncluttered floor. While you may agree to close the door again, you may not be so ready to take on the extra loads of laundry that he brings with him. Make your expectations clear. If you're making a one-time offer of laundry service because he's been bogged down in exams, be sure he understands that it really *is* one-time. Don't assume either that he will go back to doing chores that have been passed down to a sibling—but unless you're willing to run a full-service hotel, it's reasonable to set new obligations for him. Discuss your expectations *at the beginning* of the break—he's used to operating on his schedule! He may prefer to do his own laundry or other housekeeping chores that he has assumed over the last year.

The car. Unless he owns a car, your freshman will probably resume sharing the family car. Since he left, however, *someone* has gained more access to it, and unless you work out a schedule—with give-and-take on all sides—it's going to become a continuing source of irritation.

Money. Whose money will be used for spending while your child is at home? You may have set up a list of financial responsibilities for campus living, but who pays for clothes, movies, and so on when he is under your roof? It basically comes down to who visits the ATM—you or your child?

Partying. Staying out until 4 A.M. on a Wednesday night probably doesn't work into your family's schedule. It can be worse if the party's at your house, worse yet if you're not going to be home. In the latter scenario, guests tend to multiply and things can get out of hand. You know your child—you'll have to decide what kind of ground rules are necessary. Left alone for the weekend, one student and her ten friends thanked the family by repainting the outdoor furniture for the spring; a different child ruined the living room rug and gave the neighborhood a month's worth of gossip.

The boyfriend/girlfriend. If your child is going to bring a date home, don't turn the sleeping arrangements into a battleground. If you are not comfortable with the couple sharing a bedroom, be honest with him *before* the guest arrives. Consider the impact of the decision on all members of the family. Even if you know that the couple is sexually intimate, you may decide that it is sending the wrong message to younger siblings if you permit the twosome to share quarters.

REMEMBER: Do not feel uncomfortable under your own roof.

Freshman year is a time of education for both the student on campus, as well as for the parents and siblings at home. Despite your best efforts, there will still be times when your child announces, "You just don't understand." But it's all in the trying. While there may not be a written final exam for the course "Parent-Freshman Relations," you'll know your grade by the closeness and honesty of your connection.

MOVING ON: CAUGHT BETWEEN TWO WORLDS | 8

"I can remember the excitement—and exhaustion—of getting my son ready for college. I guess when we were packing everything up, though, I never thought about stuffing it all in the car again, along with whatever else he had accumulated during the year. Just before exams started, he called to say that he had taken care of it—a new storage facility near campus was going to pick most of it up. We arrived, but the van didn't. First, we sandwiched box after box into the car and drove to the storage place. Then we stuffed all the rest, plus ourselves, into the car and huffed and puffed our way home. It was 90 degrees. We realized later that the box with the dirty linens was now in storage for the summer."

Packing up a roomful of memories is never easy, whether you're leaving a house or an office. But once you close the door behind you, reluctantly or not, you tell yourself that it's time to start again. It's not like that for the college freshman. However empty his room may have been when he left your home, it was only supposed to be a temporary move—except that the place he moved to has become "home" for nine months, and now he has to get ready to move again, back to the world he left.

Who is he anyway? If you could draw a caricature at the end of the year, it would show a figure with two very large feet, one wavering above the house he's grown up in, and the other planted on campus—the reverse of what you would have drawn in the fall.

But wait a minute. Your caricature also has to show a hand reaching forward, because somewhere after the first few months of school, time began pulling the figure toward sophomore year, even as he may have tried with the other hand to hold on to the world of the child. There is a little of Peter Pan in all of us, perhaps more of him in the college freshman than we or he would like to think. His new world may be exciting, but he has to grow up to live there, and he may not be quite ready to leave his old world behind him.

WHAT HAPPENS TO OLD FRIENDS?

"Our daughter's roommate spent two hours each night on the telephone talking to a long-distance boyfriend. The line finally cleared when the romance fizzled one month into the fall term."

"My son felt weird when he brought his roommate home for Thanksgiving Break—things just didn't click with his old high school friends."

It's inevitable that friendships, even romances, will change as your student passes through freshman year. New interests, new experiences, new friends all impact on his life and previous relationships. Some old friendships may be strengthened as the connection deepens and becomes based on character and shared beliefs. Sometimes the "old group" back home may drift apart, no longer held together by proximity and shared experiences.

High school romances generally do not survive freshman year. Their demise is in some ways almost inevitable, especially if the couple does not attend the same school or one within a close commute. Distance does not necessarily make the heart grow fonder.

But as your student returns for the summer after his freshman year, how he relates to the people he left behind—his friends and romances—may influence the ease and comfort of the transition from campus to home.

Old Friendships May Change

Friendships from childhood have to withstand the test of time and distance. One parent was concerned about her son's telephone bills and road trips to friends on nearby campuses. He seemed to enjoy his campus life, so why was he holding on to his old high school buddies?

REMEMBER: These ties may be as important to your student as the relationships he may have with members of his family.

Childhood and youth were experienced with these people—bonds are strong. Your child may turn to an old friend for reassurance when life on campus throws him a curve. Peer pressure and the adjustment to college life can be softened by "touching base" with a familiar voice.

Maintaining a relationship, whether as platonic friends or serious romance, takes work. If your student didn't know it before, this is an important concept he will learn from his first year in college. Encourage him to keep in contact with old friends. With E-mail readily available on most campuses (see Chapter 6), it's easy and inexpensive to talk, via computer, to pals scattered at campuses throughout the country.

If he's worried that he or his friends no longer have anything in common, remind your child that while individual experiences may differ from school to school, college freshmen share more than one might think. Residential life is amazingly similar on most campuses—and academic demands can be scary no matter where you've chosen to go to school.

Once home, your student and his friends may need a period of adjustment as they try "to pick up where they left off." It's also understandable that he will miss his college friends and the closeness they shared. Campus friends reflect, to a certain extent, your child's selection of a place that is most compatible with his values and lifestyle. He may not have had the same options at home, and his personality may have adjusted accordingly.

Living with a group 24 hours a day is inevitably different from your child's high school experience—*but remind him that different is not better or worse, just different!* Young people often don't recognize that individuals can frequently have a wide variety of relationships based on a range of interests. If his high school friends seem markedly dissimilar to his college friends, it may be because they meet different needs.

But if a relationship has changed, if he truly no longer has anything in common with an old friend, your child will need reassurance and comfort. This can be a difficult period and can make the time at home more difficult. Encourage him to seek out new friends at his summer job or through participation in some activity that he especially enjoys. He will need peer friendships, as well as family during his vacations at home.

Realize, though, that at least for now, it's often tough to establish *new* relationships with old high school acquaintances. One student felt his high school peers could only see him as he used to be, not as who he had become after a year away at school.

Mixing Home and College Friends

Old high school friends may visit your child, or he may choose to bring a college buddy home during vacation. Sometimes it's a seamless mix; other times, the two groups don't mesh at all. Again, remind your student that he chooses friends for a variety of reasons. It's okay if the two groups don't get along. What's important is that *he* is comfortable with his friends.

Can This Romance Survive?

Despite protestations of undying love, the flames of many a high school romance flicker and die under the pressures of distance, time, and new opportunities on campus. If the decision is mutual, there may be less pain, perhaps some regret. But if your student unexpectedly receives a "Dear John" letter, it may affect his adjustment to college.

Again, your best role in this scenario is one of understanding listener—reserve all comments of "This is for the best." No one wants to hear that advice, even if you know it's true. Encourage your youngster to be active on campus—not necessarily to date, but to be around other people.

The Romance Survives, Even Thrives

No one can predict with certainty which high school romance will survive the test of time and distance. It may well be that your child has met someone special at an early age—and they grow and change in similar directions. Nonetheless, freshman year needs to be a time when both partners are open to new experiences and new friends. This does not mean that you must insist that your student date others, although it's probably a good idea to make that suggestion.

If your student's romantic partner is either still at home or on another campus, discuss your expectations *before* he leaves for school. Remind him that college is more than academics and that you want him to participate in the school's community. This can't happen if he's constantly on the road traveling to visit his beloved.

Similarly, if his partner attends the same school, the goal is for both of them to reach out and develop new friendships. By limiting his relationship to one person, even before beginning school, he may well limit the fullness of his college experience.

But as with most of college, it's his life. You can offer suggestions, but in the end, the decision will be his.

SOPHOMORE YEAR HOUSING AND ROOMMATES

"My daughter opted to take pot luck for her sophomore year roommate as long as she could be in the dorm she wanted."

"Sophomore year, my son chose to have a single room—but next door to his freshman roommate."

Your child may have more choices about where he wants to live—and with whom—as he approaches sophomore year. While most residential colleges guarantee housing for freshmen, those schools that are short on space may have limited dorm rooms available to sophomores and upperclassmen. Other schools may require students to live on campus—or at least take all or part of the university meal plans, even if the student moves off campus.

The on-campus housing for sophomores may be better, in terms of location and room size, than freshman choices. (One student, however, insisted that her college saved the best housing for first-year students to impress them and gave sophomores the least preferable dorms!) Your child may even have a greater chance of getting a single, if he prefers.

Moving Off Campus

While most schools provide on-campus housing for freshmen, housing may not be guaranteed for sophomore year. What kind of help can your child expect from the housing office if he must or prefers to move off campus? The answer varies from place to place, but in the best of circumstances there will at least be a listing of landlords whose rentals comply with local ordinances. Such a listing gives students—and parents—some assurance that the new living quarters don't pose safety or health hazards.

Some communities, bothered by noisy parties, overcrowded houses, and scarce parking, have passed ordinances restricting the number of renters per unit. Although the law may not be enforced uniformly, it is often held in reserve until neighbors think rowdy students are getting out of hand. If your child is living in this kind of setup, he runs the risk of being evicted at some point during the year. Your student should check the college housing office before signing any lease agreement. When local police are called to investigate complaints, there may not be an *arrest* record—but students should know the college's policy about putting police reports on their *school* records.

If the college housing office doesn't have a listing of available off-campus housing, your child will have to rely on word-of-mouth, school bulletin boards, newspapers ads, and real estate agencies for leads. Some students move off campus with friends, but that isn't always possible. If your child finds a new roommate by answering an ad, be sure he meets the person first and finds out about him.

As a freshman parent, you may have become less involved as the year went on, taking some solace in the living structure provided by the school. No matter how loose the rules, there is still a comforting certainty that your child is "within the walls, on campus." When he moves off campus, issues are back in your lap as well as his:

- How safe is the building and surrounding area?
- Are there working smoke detectors in the house/apartment?
- How will he get to school if he doesn't have a car? Public transportation may be available—but at all hours?
- Will he sacrifice security for accessibility to campus?
- Are there enough parking spaces for all the roommates who have cars? Where will they park if there are not?
- Is there an alarm system or other antitheft device?
- Does your homeowner's insurance cover his off-campus housing?
- If he has a roommate, will both names appear on the lease, sharing equal financial responsibility?
- If the lease is for 12 months, what will happen to the apartment during the summer? Can it be sublet? (Remember: whoever's name is on the lease is still legally responsible.)
- Who will be responsible for providing furniture? Will it be secondhand? from home? leased?
- Who will shop for and prepare the food? Does your student have the option of eating on campus?

Moving out of the dorm can seem both exciting and a further mark of independence for your child. In reality, it can be more expensive and a greater responsibility than it first appears. Sometimes students forget the convenience they took for granted in the dorm. One sophomore spent a couple of hours locked out of her apartment. She didn't take her key when she went to the laundry room, and the building manager was out to lunch.

Living off campus may be a necessity at some colleges, but at others it's an option. If there is a choice, advise your child not to make the decision lightly. Furnishing and maintaining an apartment or house may be something he's ready to handle—or perhaps not. Before signing a lease, consider:

- Will he feel isolated from activities and friends if he moves off campus? He may be less likely to return to school for a program, especially during cold winter months.
- Will he feel safe if his roommate is away for the weekend and he is alone in the apartment?
- Is he disciplined enough to control with whom and how often he parties at the apartment?

Once the decision is made to move off campus, some parents find that buying a house or apartment is less expensive in the long run than renting. Your own financial situation will influence this choice, as well as the one of whose name the property should be in. The number of children you have or will have attending school in that area, the total years involved, and the prospects for resale also come into play. Depending on location, the house or apartment may even stay in your family as a second residence.

Roommates by Choice

While your student probably didn't choose his freshman-year roommate, the choice for sophomore year and beyond is up to him. Choosing a roommate for sophomore year may be an easy decision or a source of worry. Sometimes, the choice becomes a validation of friendship, and the student not chosen is disappointed. Discourage your child, however, from making a decision too early. As one student pointed out, "The roommate you would choose in December of your freshman year is often not the same person you would prefer come May." The first year of college is a time of growth and change, and interests and friendships may vary as the year progresses.

It can be difficult for some students to talk honestly about preferences—where to room and with whom. This takes a level of interpersonal skill that may challenge even the most sophisticated undergraduate. In some ways, it was almost easier to be assigned someone—the expectations aren't as high.

Remind your student that the best roommate may be someone with compatible living and studying habits, rather than a best friend. One possible solution is to attempt to room near a large group of friends, with less emphasis on who is in any one individual room. Again, if your child is having difficulty making a decision, encourage him to talk the situation over with his resident advisor, who can offer some perspective.

THE TRANSCRIPT THICKENS

"My son called to tell us that he had decided to major in biology—although he had yet to take a single science course."

"The C in American History convinced my son never to take another course in the subject—even though it had always been one of his favorite areas of study."

Almost as soon as the acceptance letter for college arrives, people will be asking your child *the* question—"What are you going to major in?" For some, it's obvious: they enter school with a clearly defined goal. They may even have chosen a specialized college, division, or program that leaves little room for choice in classes. But for the majority, the first two years of college are a time for testing the waters. While fulfilling their academic course requirements, they are also discovering which areas they enjoy and where they might want to concentrate their interests.

As your child ends his freshman year, however, he'll be looking not only at which courses he will take in his sophomore year, but projecting for the years beyond. He'll soon have to answer the pressing question: "What are you going to do when you grow up?" But there is still a little time to decide.

Sophomore-Year Course Selections

Some schools have strong "core curriculums," academic requirements for the first two years of school, while other colleges have no requirements at all, or at least allow a wide latitude in course selection. Presumably, your child factored in the academic structure of the college when he was deciding which institution he wanted to attend.

College is a time for experimentation, and this is still important in course selection for sophomore year. Your student can sample the variety of classes his institution offers—even if he is absolutely sure that he has no intention of pursuing a particular discipline in the future. Frankly, when else will he get such an opportunity?

A note of caution, however: Check out the requirements for a major (or double major, if your child is thinking of this). He may not be able to complete the necessary courses unless he takes some specific prerequisites during his first two years. The number of requirements may also mean that he is not as free to dabble as you (and he) might think. Rather than take a potpourri of courses in sophomore year, one student—not ready to close off any options—checked out the requirements for a variety of postgraduate jobs and schools. She thus had a broad selection of courses from which to choose, but they were at least pointed in some direction. A course catalog or academic advisers should be able to provide information.

Many schools permit a student to take at least one course per academic year (some allow more) on a pass-fail basis. This is a risk-free way of trying something new. Similarly, encourage your child to audit classes—again a way to sample a subject without worrying about grades.

REMEMBER: Freshman-year grades should not necessarily influence your student's thinking about possible majors or about taking additional subjects in a particular field. Sometimes you hit a difficult teacher—don't let one professor kill a budding interest.

At the same time, be realistic. One erstwhile preengineering student switched to business when he faced the fact that poor grades were not a reflection of the teacher's talents but of his own. A high-school love of a particular subject may not be able to withstand higher-level work in the field.

Choosing a Major

At some schools, your child may have to declare a major (or concentration) by the end of his first year. Review with him *why* he has chosen a particular field and what the requirements for graduation will be. Be sure that he has factored in any possible terms away from campus (for example, internships, a semester abroad) when calculating the time frame for completing requirements for a major. Put the major in context—what relationship does the major have to future career plans, if any?

While it's reasonable to worry whether your student's choice of major will prepare him for a tight job market, there is little sense in insisting on a major he is unwilling or unable to complete. One possible compromise is a "practical" major, with an interesting "minor" if minors are offered. Some schools also allow students to major in two fields ("double major"), and the two don't even have to be related.

Remember that many professional and graduate schools no longer require specific majors—there are plenty of medical students who graduated college with a degree in English lit. On the other hand, while it is wonderful to take a broad view of undergraduate studies and major in a subject merely because it's interesting, remind your student, if he chooses a non-career-related major, that he still must factor into his course load certain classes that will fulfill graduate school requirements. He may choose a liberal arts major, but if he plans to go to medical school, then he

---

SOME MAJOR THOUGHTS ON MAJORS

1. It is *his* major, not yours. If he chooses a concentration that you studied 20 or 30 years ago, encourage him, but let him experience it for himself. Remember: The field may have changed substantially in the interim. In any case, it is his college and his program.

2. Some schools offer more flexibility in choosing a major, permitting students to construct their own programs.

3. If money is an issue, make sure your child understands that he must complete his undergraduate course offerings in a prescribed period of time. This may mean that he must choose a major and stick with it because switches can mean additional semesters.

4. Encourage your student to talk to a wide range of people before committing to a major. Not only should he discuss his choice with his academic adviser, but he should also get honest feedback on professors and course offerings from other students who are currently majoring in the same field. What sounds good on paper in the college catalogue may be sorely lacking in reality.

must figure out when and where he will take certain science courses. This may mean summer school if he can't carry these classes during the academic year—an additional expense.

SUPPOSE HE DOESN'T LIKE IT

"My son filled out all the transfer applications, paid the fees, made numerous campus visits. In the end, he decided that the school he wanted to leave wasn't so bad after all."

"My daughter was convinced that her decision to transfer was the right one—but she had to adjust to college all over again, this time without a lot of other people in the same boat."

By Thanksgiving, the vast majority of freshmen like their college. That's true even for those whose initial reaction to the school was tepid at best, as well as for those who came to the college unwillingly—a result of finances or because they had been rejected at their first-, second-, even third-choice institution. It's estimated that only 30 to 40 students out of every 1,000 decide to change schools.

There are two types of transfer students: those who planned for academic or financial reasons to attend a school for one or two years and then transfer to the institution of choice, and those students who find themselves unexpectedly unhappy for a variety of reasons. If it's clear by Winter Break that the school is not a good fit for your child, it's time to start the college application process over again.

But the decision to transfer is a lonely one. Unlike high school where everyone is going through the process at the same time, the college student is essentially on his own. He can't easily confer with his parents or the high school guidance counselor who knew him. *He* is responsible for completing the details of the application, securing the recommendations, and making sure that his transcript is sent, at the same time continuing to live and attend school in a place he now may not want to be.

What Went Wrong?

There are many reasons why your student may want to transfer.

- He wants to be closer—or further—from home.
- His grades in high school were marginal, but have improved so significantly in the first semester of college that now his application would be competitive at a more academically challenging institution.
- His economic situation has changed.
- The college is too small or large, too remote or urban, too specialized or not focused enough, and so on.
- Living arrangements or academics have been so unpleasant that it has colored his whole experience and his feelings for the school.
- He is asked to leave because of academic or disciplinary reasons.
- He wants to be closer to a love interest.
- It's just not a good fit.

Start Early and Be Persistent

Even before your child has made a final decision about transferring, check out the policies and deadlines of possible schools. While the institution will obviously be interested in your student's classes and any grades he's received, it's up to each college to decide which, if any, courses it will accept for credit. Generally, students transfer after completing one full academic year or, more rarely, after one semester.

If possible, your child should visit prospective schools and talk frankly with the admissions office about what will strengthen his application. Generally, there is a staff person assigned to handle transfer students. Most schools give greater weight to college grades, so that even if the high school record was spotty, a strong performance on the college level can make a difference. As the mother of one transfer student honestly admitted, "My son would never have been accepted at this [Ivy League] institution out of high school. His grades weren't good enough." Not only had he dramatically improved his grades, but his professors had been so impressed by his academic abilities that they were willing to write much stronger letters of recommendation than he had ever received from high school teachers.

Even if your child visited the campus while still in high school, it's wise to make another trip. He now views the school with a different perspective—through the eyes of a college freshman. He can make a more realistic comparison between his present situation and what he is now looking to change.

NOTE: Be sure that your child maintains his grades and continues to be active on his current campus even after he makes the decision to transfer. Schools are looking for students who will make a contribution to the college community—both academically and socially.

IN THE GOOD OLD SUMMERTIME

"My daughter answered an ad posted on the bulletin board at school—but they took her ice cream truck away when she didn't get her permit in time."

"We wanted our son to earn his expense money for sophomore year—he wanted us to foot his room and board bill while he waited tables at a beach resort."

Looking for a summer job is tough at best—but there are some advantages to being a college student, rather than a kid in high school, when looking for employment. Besides "greater wisdom" and maturity, college students can generally offer prospective employers a full three-month working span before they have to return to campus. Depending on your student's academic schedule, he may be home in early May, able to begin a job before Memorial Day. Those whose classes don't end until sometime in June are available to work through Labor Day— another plus for summer employment.

What kind of job is your student qualified to do? Should he look for something in his major? Where can he find suitable employment? How much can he expect to earn, or should he take a terrific *unpaid* internship? Does he need a vacation? Summer jobs, especially interesting ones, may be difficult to find. It can be the first hint of what's out there in the "real world" . . . and how will your student's summer plans impact on the family?

What Skills Does He Have to Market?

It's tough enough for college graduates to find challenging permanent jobs, so the task of finding interesting summer work can be that much harder. *But there are jobs to be had.* Some demand interpersonal skills (baby-sitter, camp counselor, waiter, salesperson); others require specialized proficiencies (lifeguard, musician); still others brute strength (construction, roadwork, gardening).

Did a year in college give your student any other skills that he can bring to the marketplace? Of course, why else did you pay all that money! He probably has developed some strong research abilities, as well as improved his organizational talents. He may also have gained some computer expertise or perhaps experience in a lab. Have him consider what courses he has taken and how they can be applied to the jobs he is seeking. An investment bank was impressed that a student had taken two economics courses his freshman year. It at least gave him a familiarity with the terms he would encounter during his summer job. Your student has also met a new group of friends and professors—which gives him a wider network of professional contacts.

He now has age and maturity on his side—there are no longer any limits on the number of hours he may work, nor is there a need for working papers.

While He's at School . . .

It's helpful to have a resume, particularly if the first contact with a prospective employer will be by mail. The career center on campus can provide guidance, but in general, he should:

- Limit the resume to one *error-free*, typewritten page.
- List "Education" first, noting that he is a first-year student; include the name of his high school and graduation date; mention any relevant courses he is taking or academic honors he has received.
- Use the dates and exact location of previous employment; include any relevant skills gained.

- Mention college extracurricular activities before those from high school, and mention the latter only if they are relevant.
- Include knowledge of a foreign language only if he is ready to speak it in an interview (unless reading ability is specified).

Some jobs require submission of a college transcript before an offer is actually made—be sure that your student arranges for one to be sent before leaving for the summer. Most employers want recommendations—again, your student should check with professors or deans early to secure their permission to use them as references.

Students who apply for interesting but unpaid internships sometimes encounter a stumbling block—a requirement that the college give credit for the summer employment. Unfortunately, many schools, while recognizing the value of these internship opportunities, will not grant course credit. If your student wants to apply for one of these jobs, he should check with his academic dean to see what accommodations the school is willing to make or if the college will send a letter explaining its policy to the prospective employer. The letter should make clear that the college recognizes the value of internships in providing important, practical experience.

When to Start Looking

The cardinal rule for summer employment is to begin the search when the leaves have barely turned color, and certainly before the first snow is on the ground! It's hard for students who are awaiting their grades for the first semester to focus on summer jobs, but the search starts early for two reasons.

First, because the budget for summer hires is usually established months ahead of time, companies and organizations may establish early deadlines for applications—this is especially true of internship programs. One student was disappointed when she failed to secure a position in Washington, D.C.—but she had missed the fall deadline for submitting her application to the political science department.

Second, your student will want to schedule appointments and interviews around college vacations. He will need to have made early contact to plan for any interviews during Spring Break.

Generally companies will first ask former employees if they wish to return.

REMEMBER: If your child wants to return to his old job, he should indicate as such at the end of the summer and then follow up by phone or mail during the fall.

Finding a Job

As many career professionals have learned, word-of-mouth or networking is the key to many good jobs. Don't overlook any possibility. One student found his summer job on Wall Street through the father of one of his kindergarten-aged sister's closest friends. Another student was hired as a lifeguard by her former coach, and a tennis player found employment through a racquet club where he had taken lessons.

Most colleges also have career counseling centers that list job opportunities and internships. Again, *go early and often* to review new entries.

When looking for employment, consider local government offices, as well as hometown corporations and businesses that may be looking for temporary help to replace vacationing employees. Consider registering with a temp agency or a youth employment service at the high school.

It may help your student secure a summer job if he offers to work whenever he is home on a break during the school year. This gives him a leg up on the competition for summer positions.

Jobs Away from Home

One of the best places to look for a summer job is on or near campus. Professors have research grants that provide slots for student employment, and local businesses often need to replace term-time student workers during the summer months. Have your child inquire at the career counseling center on campus, as well as check with his professors for employment opportunities.

Another popular option is working at a resort away from home. The prospect of spending an unsupervised summer with friends is often tempting for the freshman who may have just had an eight-month taste of independence.

But before he accepts a position on campus or otherwise away from home, you need to discuss with your child how he—and you—will feel about spending the summer apart. Be honest as you discuss:

- Will he miss not only the family, but his old friends?
- In the case of a campus job, does he need a break from the college environment?
- Is he choosing a campus job because it's a good opportunity or because a college love interest or friends are staying in the area?
- Where will he stay—and will his job cover his living expenses?

Working Hard—But Not for Pay

If your budget allows, it may make sense for your child to accept an interesting internship program. Some corporations have established summer programs that give college students the opportunity to work substantively in the field, without financial recompense. Other programs will pay a minimal salary to cover commuting expenses.

If your child cannot find an established corporate internship program but knows where he wants to work, encourage him to take the initiative and offer his services. What's the value of an unpaid internship?

- The student gets practical work experience that would otherwise be unavailable to him.
- The student can list an unpaid internship on his resume, and most employers will consider it interchangeable with paid work experience (perhaps even preferable if it's in a related profession and the paid jobs are not).

- The student is able to establish professional contacts in a field he is interested in pursuing as a career.
- The student has the opportunity to work in the field and see for himself if this is the direction he wants to continue to follow in college.

"Boring, Responsible Jobs"

For most students, *exciting* job prospects (as defined by a young adult) are limited—or if available, don't pay enough. Your child may be discouraged or depressed to return to the same job he held while in high school.

Or he may chafe at holding a "responsible" job. Even the ideal position in a student's chosen field can have drawbacks when he finds that, for now, everyone else there is older than he is. After a week as a paralegal, one student complained to her mother that "it would be more fun" if she had taken a waitress job in a local resort. Parental talk of resume building was of no comfort.

Part of the unhappiness comes from having to adjust to returning home after the freedom and excitement of campus life. It really doesn't matter where you live—students from big cities also complain that the "town is boring, there's nothing to do!"

Other Summer Options

Travel, volunteer work, or summer school (or a combination of all three) are other possibilities to consider if your child can't or doesn't need to find a job. Many campus career counseling offices and individual academic departments have information on student programs in this country and abroad. Again, check early as many of these programs have early application deadlines. Often there are travel and study grants available. The summer between freshman and sophomore year is not a bad time to consider one of these programs. Travel is broadening and provides your child with the opportunity to test himself in new and demanding circumstances. There is also less pressure at this time to start building a resume.

TIP: If your student is planning to travel abroad, whether for pleasure or study, be sure he gets an international student I.D. card. It will entitle him to discounts on admissions to museums and other places of interest.

And How Does His Job Affect You?

Whatever summer job or program your student chooses, it will undoubtedly affect your family life. As one parent pointed out, "His job is costing me a fortune!" Sure it was great that the student had gotten a terrific corporate job, but his college wardrobe of jeans and T-shirts did not satisfy the office dress code of suits, dress shirts, ties, etc. Even if your child intends to pay for these added expenses out of his salary, you may be forced to "foot the bill" until the first paycheck arrives—which can take several weeks.

If you are hoping to take a family vacation, your student may have other ideas or obligations. You will have to coordinate your plans not only with his job schedule, but also with any campus responsibilities he might have. Sophomores often return to school early in order to help with freshman orientation programs.

Does He Need a Vacation?

If college, according to those phone calls from campus to home, sounds suspiciously like one party after another, you can sympathize with the mother who wondered aloud why her son now needed a vacation. "A vacation from what?" she asked. But in a more charitable mood, remember that freshman year is physically and emotionally exhausting and that the end of the academic year can be especially grueling.

If possible, suggest that your student take a few days off before beginning a summer job and another few days to organize himself and his belongings before returning to school. He'll need the time to shift gears successfully.

REVERSING THE TRIP

"My daughter was offered a ride home—but there was only room in the car for one duffel bag."

"A van organized by students on campus was dropping my child's stuff off, but the meeting place turned out to be a busy city street—and there was a parade going on!"

What goes up must come down—what goes into that dorm room must come out and go somewhere. Under the best of circumstances, moving from one place to another can be draining. In the case of the college student, it is that much more difficult because it comes at the end of an emotion-filled year, in the midst of exams, and perhaps during the season's first heat wave.

Much to the chagrin of parents, it's not uncommon for freshmen to postpone packing until the very last moment. After all, they've never been through this before, probably don't know how long it takes, and may not even be sure what they're going to do with all the "stuff" that's accumulated. But more than any of that, there's an emotional tug. As one girl sobbed, "I can't deal with this. This room has been my home for eight months!" That's the tough part for you because it sums up in a nutshell what's been going on for the year.

You may be anxious to see your child again, but he may not be responding as quickly as you would like to your hints about packing up. Sure he still loves you and your home, but now he's come to love another place too. Some freshmen even make plans to "vacation" (again!) with classmates before heading home—a last-minute grasp at bonding with new friends. While it's tough to put your own emotions on the back burner, patience may result in a happier summer!

Bring? Send? Store?

For the child who overpacked or accumulated too many extra possessions during the year, moving out of the dorm can be a monumental task.

REMEMBER: The date for vacating the dorm is nonnegotiable and can, in fact, come within a day after exams end.

SHORTCUTS HOME

Planning ahead was the key to getting ready for college; more planning is the key to closing down for the summer.

1. Decide early on how and when your child is coming home.

2. Be realistic about how much he can bring home with him: Will it fit? Does he need it?

3. Suggest that he bring home during the year what he no longer needs on campus.

4. If you visit, bring an (empty) bag along and take some un-needed clothes home with you.

5. Ship items home as they are no longer needed.

6. If your child's belongings will be driven to a central location near your home, check the area ahead of time: Is there easy access in and out? Can you park close enough to make carrying everything possible?

7. Encourage your child to pack some of his things **before** he gets immersed in the pressures of finals.

8. Find out whether local thrift organizations pick up unwanted clothes and the like from campus at the end of the year.

You may not have the luxury of moving out leisurely, days after the end of school. It's not unusual to see parents packing the stairwells again, this time carrying boxes down, while many students are still in the midst of studying and others haven't begun to pack.

The only definite in a possibly chaotic situation is that the room will have to be emptied. The contents can be brought home, sent home, or left in storage. Which one, or combination, you choose can depend on:

- *Your child's own travel arrangements.* If he's driving home alone, with plenty of room in the car, your options are wide open. If he lives close enough to the campus that you or he can make several trips, space in the car won't make a difference. If he's flying, or riding in a car full of people, he won't be able to bring all his gear with him. If he's not coming straight home, he may not want to risk leaving everything in the car along the way.

- *His summer needs.* Depending on the weather at home and how soon your child will be going back to school in the fall, he may never use heavier clothing and bedding until he gets back to campus. He may never miss his computer, phone, other electronic equipment, even extra linens.

- *Cost and convenience of options.* Bringing everything home with you in a car is the least expensive option. Shipping or storage will be costlier, but either one may also be more convenient. Note, however, that storage facilities may not be easily accessible (particularly if your child doesn't have a car), whereas some shipping services will pick up from campus. Check the price and service provided by the various packing alternatives (see Chapter 1).

A Word About Storage

The easiest, least expensive way to move out of the dorm is to put everything in the car and drive it home yourself. After all, you don't need boxes, dirty laundry can be stuffed in those by-now familiar clear garbage bags, and unwanted possessions don't have to be sorted out right then. On the other hand, your child will probably bring most of it back again in the fall, and that may be a task you don't want to face again.

Whatever the logistics, storage on or near campus can make a great deal of sense. Rather than pay to send a bike home (boxed and disassembled), one student kept it at a bike shop for the summer; the fee was offset by what it would have cost to ship it back and forth, and the bicycle was tuned up for the fall. Another freshman brought clothes and linens to a local dry cleaner and then took advantage of free box storage for three months. The family who had had a car driven across country saved the money of a return trip by keeping it at a classmate's nearby home until the fall.

Some campuses provide storage in the dorm assigned to your child for sophomore year; others have central storage. Your child might choose to use an outside storage facility

STORAGE TIPS

Once the decision is made to store some of your child's belongings, advise him to:

1. Keep a clear inventory of what is stored to avoid rebuying what seems to be "missing" when packing up at home for the return trip to school.

2. Make a duplicate of any key and put it in a safe place; write down the combination of a lock instead of just committing it to memory.

3. Check the insurance included with the rental. If it doesn't seem sufficient, additional coverage can be purchased for a minimum fee. Also check your homeowner's policy to see if items in storage are covered.

4. Back up computer files on a separate disk—and do not store with the computer.

5. Launder/dry clean clothes before storing them.

6. Check the temperature of the facility if you are storing fragile items (bottom floors will be cooler).

7. Remove everything from storage by the date specified in the contract.

8. Don't store what you can't afford to lose!

instead, either by himself or with a group of friends. In the latter, space in a warehouse is divided into "rooms" that are rented and locked; the number of students per room is determined simply by how much stuff they have and whether it fits. Check notices on student bulletin boards and ads in the campus newspaper, or call a local moving company for suggestions of reputable storage businesses. Management of the facility will not take responsibility for stolen goods, so insurance is important. In most locations, it can be purchased at the time of storage, but you should also find out whether your homeowner's insurance provides coverage.

Although there is no foolproof—or burglarproof—system, local police suggest using facilities that have security patrols or require access codes to enter storage lots. On-site managers and fences may be a deterrent to theft, but they don't guarantee security. Remember too that if a company has more than one site, security may not be the same at each of them.

When you're deciding which storage facility to use, also check the location and compare the costs. What has been the experience of upperclassmen with various places? Find out the packaging requirements—must everything be boxed? Are there any guidelines for fragile items?

You'll want to know whether there is pickup from the dorm or whether your child will have to do the transporting. If he doesn't have a car or access to one, discuss how he will get his stuff to the storage company. In the fall, how will he get the items back to the dorm? Is there a definite pickup date? any penalty for missing the date? If the date is after school begins, be sure your child can start the semester without the items he put in storage. If the date is before he plans on returning to campus, then he will have to arrange for someone else to get his things.

The summer after freshman year will continue the period of transition you and your child have been living through since he received that high school diploma. As he moves into sophomore year, he will assume more responsibility for his decisions and his future. You may see his academic, and perhaps his career, pathway beginning to take shape. He may choose a "resume-building" summer job, hang out at the beach, travel, or take classes—but in any case, this summer will continue to be a time of change.

Your child may chafe at the bit: He's had more than eight months on his own. As a parent, you'll walk a delicate tightrope, generally keeping tongue in check. Encourage his independence, offer support, cheer as he makes intelligent adult decisions, and then watch incredulously while he acts like a baby on other occasions. He's not quite an adult—not still a child. He needs you, but it's a balancing act, as you serve as parent, friend, mentor, and (often silent, but vigilant) watchdog.

SOME FINAL THOUGHTS

Time goes faster when you are older. It seems like just yesterday you took your baby to school at the start of kindergarten, and before you know it, he's finishing his freshman year of college. In some ways, the first year of college is much like the first year of life—a time when you see tremendous, seemingly overnight changes. In that momentous first year of being, you saw your child go from a helpless newborn to a walking, talking personality kid! Similarly, the first year of college is a time of incredible emotional and intellectual development. The adolescent you delivered to campus in September is not the same person who arrives home, albeit with bags of dirty laundry, on your doorstep for the summer.

Nor are you the same parent. You've had to learn to let go. You've learned throughout this year that your student's choices may not be the same ones you would make for him, but in most cases, it is *his life* and his judgment you must respect. You will be developing a new relationship with this young adult, one based on mutual respect, as well as love. He still very much needs you, but on different terms.

Sometimes we'd like to keep them small and protect them from harm and hurt. But with strong, open lines of communication, lots of love, and confidence in his strengths and abilities, you will have given your child not only a college education, but also the life skills he will need. This next stage in your parent-child relationship can be every bit as exciting and meaningful as the early years. Enjoy!

Appendix A
WHAT YOU TOOK AND
WHERE YOU PACKED IT

WHAT YOU TOOK	WHERE YOU PACKED IT	WHAT YOU TOOK	WHERE YOU PACKED IT
Clothing			
Underwear		Shorts	
Slips		Sweat Suits	
Bras		Bathing Suit	
Pajamas		Socks	
Robe		Shoes	
Dresses		Boots	
T-shirts		Bedroom Slippers	
Blouses/Shirts		Shower Shoes	
Skirts		(flip-flops)	
Sweaters		Raincoat	
Blazer/Jackets		Winter Coat	
Ties		Windbreaker	
Slacks		Hats/Gloves	
Jeans		Other	

WHAT YOU TOOK	WHERE YOU PACKED IT	WHAT YOU TOOK	WHERE YOU PACKED IT
Jewelry			
Electronics			
Alarm		Camera/Film	
Calculator		Fan	
Stereo/CD Player		Coffeepot	
Television		Microwave Oven	
VCR		Popcorn Popper	
Video Game(s)		Hot Pot	
Radio		Iron	
Walkman Radio		Extension Cords	
Telephone		Electric Adapters/ Converters/ Power Strips	
Telephone Answering Machine			
		Other	
Computer			
Hard Drive		Software	
Monitor		Information Manuals	
Printer		Telephone Numbers for Help	
Surge Protector			
Reference Manuals			
Dictionary		Thesaurus	
Foreign Language Dictionary		Other	
Bedding			
Mattress Pad		Pillows	
Sheets		Towels	
Pillowcases		Washcloths	
Blanket(s)		Hand Towels	
Comforter		Bedrests	
Duvet		Other	

WHAT YOU TOOK	WHERE YOU PACKED IT	WHAT YOU TOOK	WHERE YOU PACKED IT
Sports Equipment			
Tennis Racquet		Frisbee	
Golf Clubs		Swimming Goggles	
Free Weights		Other	
Baseball Glove			
Room Accessories			
Lamp(s)		Posters	
Specialty Lightbulbs		Calendar	
Fan		Storage Crates	
Wastebasket		Photo Albums	
Bulletin Board		Yearbook	
Pictures/Frames		Other	
Laundry			
Laundry Bags		Roll of Quarters	
Detergent/Stain Remover/ Fabric Softener		Iron and Ironing Board	
Miscellaneous			
Hangers		Backpack	
Cosmetics		Security Lock Box	
Shower Caddy		Coffee Mug, Bowl, Utensils	
Hair Dryer		Cleaning Equipment	
Musical Instruments		Stationery/ Stamps	

Appendix B
NAMES AND NUMBERS

	NAME/ADDRESS	NUMBER
Basic Information		
Student Phone (Best Time for Regular Calls)		
Mail		
Packages		
E-Mail		
Work		
Roommate	Home Campus	
Roommate's Parents		
Resident Advisor		
Dean of Students		
Bursar		
Financial Aid		
Other		

	NAME/ADDRESS	NUMBER
Banking		
Bank Contact		
Checking Account		
Savings Account		
Bank ABA Code		
ATM PIN Number		
Credit Card Number		
To Report Lost/Stolen Card		
Health Care		
Insurance Contact		
Health Center/Infirmary		
At-Home Doctors:		
Primary Care		
Dentist		
Eye Doctor		
Accommodations		
Hotel/Motel		
Restaurants		
Care Packages		
Campus/Off-Campus Services:		
Bakery		
Florist		
Groceries		
Mail Services		
Cars		
Insurance Contact	Phone Policy #	
Road Service	Phone Policy #	
Storage Facility		
Storage Key Location		
Bicycle Shop		

Appendix C
DATEBOOK

EVENT	
Dates	
Orientation	
Classes Start	
Break(s)	
Exams	
Vacations	
Parents' Weekend	
Classes End	
Other	
Train/Plane/Bus Schedules	
Airline Ticket Numbers	

Appendix D
CLASS SCHEDULE

COURSE	DAY(S)	TIME(S)

Appendix E
COLLEGE 800 DIRECTORY

Here are some of the 800 numbers used most often.

APPAREL, LINENS, HOUSEWARES

Coming Home	1-800-345-3696
The Company Store	1-800-285-3936
Hold Everything	1-800-421-2264
J. Crew	1-800-562-0258
J.C. Penny	1-800-222-6161
Land's End	1-800-356-4444
Lillian Vernon	1-800-285-5555
L.L. Bean	1-800-221-4221
Patagonia	1-800-638-6464
Tweed's	1-800-999-7997
Victoria's Secret	1-800-888-8200

COMPUTERS

Gateway Computer	1-800-846-2000
IBM Direct	1-800-426-3333

FINANCIAL AID

Federal Student Financial Aid Information Center	1-800-433-3243

SHIPPING

Airborne Express	1-800-247-2676
DHL	1-800-225-5345
Federal Express	1-800-238-5355
UPS	1-800-742-5877
U.S. Post Office	1-800-222-1811

TELEPHONE SERVICES

AT&T	1-800-222-0300
MCI	1-800-950-5555
Sprint	1-800-877-7746

TRANSPORTATION
Airlines

American	1-800-433-7300
Continental	1-800-525-0280
Delta	1-800-221-1212
Midway Airlines	1-800-446-4392
Northwest Airlines	1-800-225-2525
Southwest Airlines	1-800-435-9792
United	1-800-241-6522
U.S. Air	1-800-428-4322
TWA	1-800-221-2000

Buses

Greyhound Bus Line	1-800-231-2222
Short Line Bus System	1-800-631-8405

Rail

Amtrak	1-800-USA-RAIL

Appendix F
SEXUAL HARASSMENT

[Here is an example of a college sexual-harassment policy. It is from SUNY Purchase College's Policy for Students Handbook.*]*

Harassment on the basis of sex is a violation of the Civil Rights Act of 1964 (Section 703 of Title VII), and sexual harassment in any form will not be tolerated at the college.

I. Definition

Sexual harassment is defined as: unwelcome sexual advances, requests for sexual favors, and other verbal or physical conduct of a sexual nature when:

a. submission to such conduct is made either explicitly or implicitly a term or condition of an individual's employment,

b. submission or rejection of such conduct by an individual is used as the basis for employment decisions affecting such individual, or

c. such conduct has the purpose or effect of interfering with an individual's work performance or creating an intimidating, hostile, or offensive work environment.

This policy applies equally to employees and students, male and female. Those who feel they have been victims of such discrimination should contact the affirmative action officer, or the vice president for student affairs. Pursuing a complaint on campus does not rescind the right to file with an outside enforcement agency such as the State Division of Human Rights.

II. Sexual Orientation

The Governor's Executive Order No. 28 prohibits all state agencies from discriminating on the basis of sexual orientation in the provision of any services or benefits by a state agency and in any matter relating to employment by the state.

a. Sexual orientation is defined as a private preference of an individual protected by Executive Order No. 28 for heterosexuality, homosexuality, or bisexuality; or a history of such preference; or an identification with having such a preference.
b. Harassment on the basis of sexual orientation is judged against the same criteria as those for sexual harassment, and protection applies to students, as well as to employees, to males as well as to females.
c. Complaints may be made to the affirmative action officer/personnel director or the vice president for student affairs. This does not rescind a person's right to file a complaint with the Governor's Office of Employee Relations.

[Reprinted courtesy of SUNY Purchase College.]

Appendix G
ACTIVITIES GROUPS

[This is a list of some of the most common activity groups on college campuses today. It is from *Connections: Student Organizations at the University of Pennsylvania, 1993–94.*]

UNIVERSITY OF PENNSYLVANIA
1993–94 Activities Council Organizations
These groups are recognized and most are funded by the Student Activities Council (SAC), the branch of the undergraduate student government which is responsible for overseeing the campuswide activities program. There are a number of other organizations which register with the Office of Student Life Activities and Facilities but do not belong to the SAC. Information on all of these groups may be obtained at the Houston Hall Information Desk (898–INFO) or from Penninfo, the University's on-line information system. All groups welcome new members, graduate and undergraduate alike.

Academic Societies in Engineering
Accounting Society
ACELA (Latino students)
ADEPEP (Puerto Rican students)
AIESEC (International business)

Alpha Phi Omega (service)
Alternate Spring Break
Amateur Radio Club
American Marketing Association
Amnesty International at Penn

Amorphous Jugglers
Armenian Club
Arts House Dance Company
Arts House Theater
Ayalah (Israeli folk dancing)
Balalaika Orchestra
Ballroom Dance Club
Bands
Best Buddies
BIG-C (Bicultural InterGreek
Council.)
Biochemistry Club
BioMedical Research Society
Black Student League
Black Wharton Undergrad. Assoc.
Bloomers (women's comedy)
Campuses Against Cancer
Caribbean-American Student Assoc.
Chemistry Club
Chess Club
Chinese Students Association
Choral Society/Choir
Chord On Blues (men's a capella)
Circle K
College Bowl
College Republicans
Comic Collectors Club
Community Kids
Commuters
Connaissance (lecture bureau)
Counterparts (coed a capella)
Course Review
Debate Council
Dixon House
Drug and Alcohol Resource Team
Economics Society
Education Society
Entrepreneurial Club
Environmental & Recycling
    Group
Event Horizon (science fiction mag.)
Finance Club
FLASH (sexual health peer educ.)
Glee Club

Gospel Choir
Greek Club
Habitat for Humanity
Hawaii Club
Highball (humor magazine)
Hillel
Hong Kong Club at Penn
The Inspiration (coed a capella)
Interfraternity Council
Intl. Affairs Assoc (Model UN)
International Relations Association
International Students Association
Intervarsity Christian Fellowship
Intuitons (experimental theater)
Irish Club
Italian Society
Japan Cultural Society
Jazz Ensemble
Jewish Social Action Committee
John Marshall Pre-Law Society
John Morgan Pre-Health Society
Kite and Key (campus service)
Korean Students Association
Lesbian, Gay, Bisexual Alliance
Lubavitch Student Association
Management ampersand
Technology Club
Management Club
Mask and Wig (men's comedy)
MECHA (Chicano students)
Mosaic (Asian issues)
Musicians Against Homelessness
New Student Orientation
Nursing Student forum
Newman Council
Off the Beat (coed a capella)
Outing Club
Pakistan Society
Panhellenic Council
Passport (intl. magazine)
Penn Consumers Board
Penn Dance
Penn Dixie (Dixieland jazz)
Penn Players (theater)

Penn Political Union
Penn Pro Choice
Penn Review (literary magazine)
Penn Singers (light opera)
Penn Six-5000 (men's a capella)
Penn Transfers
Penn Triangle (engineering mag.)
Penn World Review
PENNpals
Penny Loafers (coed a capella)
Philomathean Society
Phi Sigma Pi
Psychology Society
Punch Bowl (humor magazine)
Quadramics (theater)
Quaker Notes (women's a capella)
RAP (Reach a Peer) Line
Real Estate Club
The Record (yearbook)
Social Respons. in Business
Society of Auto. Engineers
Soc. of Hispanic Prof. Engineers
Society of Women Engineers
South Asia Society
SPARKS (philanth. dance troupe)
Sports Club Council
Stimulus Education (tutoring)
Stimulus Children's Theater
Student Natl. Medical Soc.
Student Pugwash
Students for Asian Affairs
Stud. Tgthr. Agst. Acquaint. Rape
Symphony Orchestra
Taiwanese Society
Univ. City Hospitality Coalition
University Television
Vietnamese club
Wharton Account (business mag.)
Wharton Women
Wind Ensemble
Without a Net (improv. comedy)
Women's Alliance
WQHS (AM radio station)
Writer's Guild

WXPN Sports (FM radio station)
Young America's Foundation

ATHLETICS
Varsity Sports
Baseball (M)
Basketball (M & W)
Crew (M & W)
Cross County (M & W)
Fencing (M & W)
Field Hockey (W)
Football (M)
Golf (M)
Gymnastics (W)
Lacrosse (M & W)
Lightweight Football (M)
Soccer (M & W)
Softball (W)
Squash (M & W)
Swimming (M & W)
Tennis (M & W)
Track (M & W)
Volleyball (W)
Wrestling (M)

Intramural Sports
2 on 2 Coed Basketball
Basketball
Coed Football
Coed Soccer
Coed Softball
Coed Volleyball
Football
Free Throw
Soccer
Softball
Swimming
Squash
Tennis
Tennis—Mixed Doubles
Track and Field
Volleyball

Club Sports
Aikido

Badminton	Karate
Baseball	Lacrosse
Basketball	Pennguinettes (sync. swim)
Bicycling	Racquetball
Bowling	Rifle and Pistol
Cricket	Rugby (M & W)
Equestrian	Sailing
Frisbee	Skiing
Golf	Tennis
Gymnastics	Volleyball
Ice Skating	Water Polo
Ice Hockey (M & W)	

[Reprinted courtesy of the University of Pennsylvania.]

Appendix H
NEW-STUDENT ORIENTATION EVENTS SCHEDULED FOR PARENTS

[This appendix contains a typical schedule of activities for parents during New Student Orientation.]

THURSDAY, AUGUST 26, 1993

8:30 and 11:00 A.M. Meeting for parents of Trinity College entering students with Dr. Richard White, Dean of Trinity College, and Ms. Janet Smith Dickerson, Vice President for Student Affairs. Page Auditorium, West Campus.

9:00 A.M. Meeting for parents of new students enrolling in the School of Engineering. Address by Dean Earl Dowell and Associate Dean Marion Shepard. Griffith Film Theater, Bryan Center, West Campus.

10:00–11:00 A.M. Parents' Reception with Religious Life Staff, Duke Chapel Basement Lounge, West Campus. (Enter on the Bryan Center side.)

10:00 A.M. Parents may choose to attend one of the following preprofessional meetings:

Parent's preview to premedical and other health professions. Question and answer session with the Director of Health Professions Advising. Griffith Film Theater, Bryan Center, West Campus.

Parents' preview to prebusiness advising and resources available to students through the Career Development Center. Page Auditorium, West Campus.

11:00 A.M.   Parents' preview to prelaw advising. Griffith Film Theater, Bryan Center, West Campus

11:30 A.M.–**1:00** P.M.   Parents and their students are invited to an informal light-lunch reception hosted by President Nannerl O. Keohane on the main West Campus academic and residential quadrangles. There is no official program followed at this reception. New students and their parents will have an opportunity to meet the President, faculty, and administrators. These individuals can be located at each of the following color-coded tables:

Trinity College—Red
Engineering—Green
Student Affairs—Pink
University Administration—Yellow
President Keohane—Blue

In the event of inclement weather, the reception will be canceled. Parents and students find that following the reception, it is a propitious time for parents to begin their departure for home.

1:00–4:00 P.M.   Ms. Jane Clark Moorman, Director of Counseling and Psychological Services (CAPS), will be available for consultation in Suite 214 Page Building. Students and their parents may confer with Ms. Moorman and members of her staff concerning any personal concerns about which CAPS should be made aware.

1:00–4:00 P.M.   The Director of Student Health will be available for consultation in the Student Health Office (Pickens Family Medicine Center, 2100 Erwin Road). Students and their parents may confer with the Director concerning any health problems about which the Student Health Office should be made aware.

[Reprinted courtesy of Duke University.]

Appendix I
PARENTS' WEEKEND SCHEDULE

Here is a sample Parents' Weekend schedule.

Parents' Weekend 1994

Duke University invites you to Parents' Weekend 1994, November 4-6. This weekend provides an opportunity for you to visit with your sons and daughters, their friends and professors, as well as share in the Duke experience.

There is something for everyone! The weekend is full of activities from open classes to sporting events. Join us as Students for a Day, tour the Duke University Primate Center, and meet President Nannerl Keohane. Plan now to attend seminars on a broad range of topics, including Generation X, multiculturalism, and the major/career connection.

Football fans can cheer the Blue Devils as they confront the Virginia Cavaliers in Wallace Wade Stadium, while basketball enthusiasts can catch a glimpse of the 1994-95 basketball team in action during the Blue-White Scrimmage in Cameron Indoor Stadium.

Others may explore the culture of the University community by visiting the Duke University Museum of Art or by attending the Duke Drama presentation of "The House of Blue Leaves." Hear the Duke Wind Symphony and the Duke Chorale in their Showcase Concert or listen to the gospel sound of the Modern Black Mass Choir.

Parents' Weekend is a special time for parents and students. Discover what the University has to offer, and learn about the organizations, people, and places that have become important to your son or daughter.

Here is a preview of festivities and information that will be helpful to you as you plan your visit to Duke University. Use the form in this brochure to register. We're expecting you!

Material condensed from Parents' Weekend *brochure. [Reprinted courtesy of Duke University.]*

EVENT INFORMATION
Room Capacities

In anticipation of another successful Parents' Weekend, a wide variety of classes and activities have been scheduled. All are on a first come first serve basis, so in the event of overcrowding, please feel free to select an alternative.

*Locations and/or Topics are subject to change. Please refer to updated schedules in Registration packet upon check-in.

FRIDAY, NOVEMBER 4

Registration
Bryan Center Lobby   9 a.m.–5. p.m.

Study Abroad Information Table
Bryan Center Lobby   9 a.m.–5. p.m.

Duke University Museum of Art
East Campus   Open 9 a.m.–5 p.m.

Classes Open to Parents
East and West Campuses

School of the Environment Classes
Levine Research Science Center   8 a.m.–12 noon

School of the Environment Open House
Levine Research Science Center   10 a.m.–11:30 a.m.

Fuqua School Information Session and Tour
Fuqua School of Business   10 a.m.–12 noon

"Being a Parent to an Emerging Adult: Letting Go and Holding It Together."
Mary Lou Williams Cultural Center
02 Union West   11 a.m.–11:50 a.m.

Divinity School Hosts Parents for Refreshments
Alumni Memorial Commons Room
115 New Divinity   11 a.m.–12 noon

"Writing Through Duke and Beyond"
Duke Art Museum's North Gallery   11 a.m.–12 noon

"Introduction to the Old Testament"
Centenary Lecture Hall, Room
022 New Divinity   12 noon–12:50 p.m.

"Alcohol at Duke: The Real Story"
Mary Lou Williams Cultural Center
02 Union West   12 noon–12:50 p.m.

Hospitality Table hosted by Friends of the Gardens
Sarah P. Duke Gardens   12 noon–4 p.m.

Student for a Day
Griffith Film Theater, Bryan Center,
West Campus   1 p.m.–2 p.m. and
                                                        3 p.m.–3:50 p.m.
                                                        Also Sat. Nov 5 at
                                                        10 a.m.

**Student for a Day Lecture 1: "Race Matters:
Our Nation's Fiction"**
Griffith Film Theater, Bryan Center,
West Campus   1 p.m.–2 p.m.
Karla F.C. Holloway (Ph.D., Michigan State)
  is Professor of English and
  African American Literature.

"The Major/Career Connection: Is It a Myth?"
Centenary Lecture Room, 022 New Divinity
  (new wing of the Divinity School)   2 p.m.–2:50 p.m.

"Eating Disorders"
May Lou Williams
Cultural Center
02 West Union   2 p.m.–2:50 p.m.

**The Phi Kappa Psi James Valvano Memorial
Celebrity Auction**
Bryan Center Walkway (Inside the
  Bryan Center in the event of rain)   2 p.m.–4 p.m.

Financial Aid Open House
2106 Campus Drive   2 p.m.–4 p.m.

**"Treasures and Technology: A Guided Tour
of Perkins Library"**
Perkins Library Lobby   2 p.m.–3 p.m. and
                                                        3 p.m.–4 p.m.

"History and Traditions of Duke University"
110 Gray Building, Old Divinity   3 p.m.–3:50 p.m.

**Student for a Day Lecture 2: "Toads, Worms,
and Brains"**
Griffith Film Theater, Bryan Center,
West Campus   3 p.m.–3:50 p.m.
Stephen Nowicki (Ph.D., Cornell) is Associate
  Professor of Zoology, Neurobiology, and
  Experimental Psychology

"Opportunities for Study Abroad"
Breedlove Room, 204 Perkins Library   3:00 p.m.–4:00 p.m.

**Questions and Answers with President
Keohane and Others**
Griffith Film Theater, Bryan Center,
West Campus   4 p.m.–4:50 p.m.

President's Reception
Von Canon Hall, Lower level of the
Bryan Center, West Campus   5 p.m.–5:50 p.m.

Parents' Weekend Buffet Dinner
The Great Hall, West Campus   6 p.m.–8 p.m.

Shabbat Services and Dinner by Duke Hillel
Hillel House, 311 Alexander Avenue,
Central Campus   6 p.m.–9 p.m.

The Navigators Meeting
Room 201 Flowers (the building to the left
of the Chapel)   7:30 p.m.–9 p.m.

James Galway, Flutist
Page Auditorium   8 p.m.

**Duke Drama Performance: "The House of
Blue Leaves"**
R.J. Reynolds Industries Theater,
Bryan Center   8 p.m. Also,
                                               Saturday, 8 p.m.

Writers Read
Perkins Library Rare Book Room   8 p.m.

Freewater Films: "The Snapper"
Griffith Film Theater, Bryan Center   7 p.m.–9:30 p.m.

SATURDAY, NOVEMBER 5

Registration
Bryan Center Lobby   9 a.m.–12 noon

Meeting with the Pre-Law Advisor
136 Social Sciences   9 a.m.–9:50 a.m.

The Pre-Major Advising Center Open House
Pre-Major Advising Center, East Campus   9 a.m.–10:30 a.m.

**"Redefining 'American': the Changing Cultures
of Duke"**
Breakfast and Multicultural Discussion
Spectrum House, West Campus
Residential Quadrangle   9 a.m.–10:50 a.m.

"Preparing Students for the Future: How the Women's Center and the Women's Studies Program Support Student Development"
Women's Center (between SAE and
Roundtable on West Campus)   9 a.m.–9:50 a.m.

Wesley Fellowship
Location to be announced   10 a.m.

Undergraduate Admissions Information Session
Undergraduate Admissions Office,
2138 Campus Drive   10 a.m.

Student for a Day Lecture 3: "Genocide: Perpetrators and Rescuers"
Griffith Film Theater   10 a.m.–11 a.m.
Claudia Koonz (Ph.d., Rutgers) is Associate
Professor of History.

Public Policy Continental Breakfast and Panel Discussion
Fleishman Comons, Sanford Institute,
Science Drive   10 a.m.–12 noon

Student Organization Fair
Middle level of the Bryan Center   10:45 a.m.–12 noon

Duke University Museum of Art
East Campus   Open 11 a.m.–5 p.m.

Community Service Panel and Discussion
La Barr Auditorium, 139 Social Sciences   11 a.m.–12 noon

"Alcohol at Duke: New Opportunities"
Women's Center, 126 Few Fed
(Between SAE and Roundtable on
West Campus)   11 a.m.–11:50 a.m.

Engineering Seminar featuring Gary W. Dickinson
Auditorium, Room 103, Bryan Neurobiology
Building (on Research Drive across from
the Engineering Building)   11 a.m.–12 noon

Alumni/ae Sponsored Barbecue
Cameroon Indoor Stadium
Two hours prior to the football game

The Engineering Barbecue
Engineering Side Lawn   12 noon–1 p.m.

Hospitality Table hosted by Friends of the Gardens
Sarah P. Duke Gardens   12 noon–4 p.m.

Football — Duke vs. Virginia
Wallace Wade Stadium   1:30 p.m.

Basketball — Blue and White Scrimmage
Cameron Indoor Stadium   T.B.A. (after the
                                             football game)

Parents' Weekend Buffet Dinner
The Great Hall, West Campus   6 p.m.–8 p.m.

Quadrangle Pictures: "The Paper"
Griffith Film Theater, Bryan Center   7 p.m.–9:30 p.m.

**Duke Drama Performance "The House of
Blue Leaves"**
R.J. Reynolds Industries Theater   8 p.m.–10 p.m.

Showcase Concert
Duke Chapel, West Campus   8 p.m.–10 p.m.

Mary Lou Williams Jazz Festival
Page Auditorium, West Campus   8 p.m.

Writers Read
Thomas Room, Lilly Library   8 p.m.

SUNDAY, NOVEMBER 6

Black Campus Ministry Prayer Breakfast
Multi-purpose Center, Oregon Street,
Central Campus   8 a.m.–10 a.m.

**"Today's Young Adults—What's Happening with
Generation X?"**
Conversaton with Vice President Dickerson
and Dean Willimon
022 New Divinity   9:45 a.m.–10:45 a.m.

Discussion with Oli Jenkins
211 Old Divinity Building   9:45 a.m.–10:45 a.m.

Holy Eucharist Service and Brunch
Episcopal Center, 505 Alexander Drive   10 a.m.

Catholic Mass
Page Auditorium   10:30 a.m.–11:30 a.m.

Hillel Foundation Brunch
Von Canon Suites A, B, C, Bryan Center   10:30 a.m.–12:30 p.m.

Service of Worship
Duke University Chapel   11 a.m.–12 noon

Duke University Museum of Art
East Campus   Open 12 noon–5 p.m.

Guided Tour of the Gardens
Sarah P. Duke Gardens   2 p.m.–3 p.m.

**Modern Black Mass Choir Fall Concert
and Reception**
   Page Auditorium   3:30 p.m.

**Quadrangle Pictures
"The Paper"**
   Griffith Film Theater   8 p.m.–10 p.m.

INDEX